CARLO MARIA MARTINI

BIBLICAL MEDITATIONS

CARLO MARIA MARTINI

THE APOSTLES
MEN OF PEACE AND
RECONCILIATION

MEDITATIONS

COVENTRY
PRESS

Published in Australia by
Coventry Press
www.coventrypress.com.au
33 Scoresby Road Bayswater VIC 3153
an imprint of Freedom Publishing Books
www.freedompublishingbooks.com.au

ISBN 9780648230397

First published in Italy under the title *Uomini di pace e di riconcilizione. Meditazioni sulla coscienza missionaria*, [Men of peace and reconciliation. Meditations on missionary consciousness] by Edizioni Borla, Rome 1985.

Re-published by
©2017 Edizioni San Paolo s.r.l,
Piazza Soncino 5 - 20092 Cinisello Balsamo (Milano) - ITALIA
www.edizionisanpaolo.it

Catalogue-in-Publication entry is available from the National Library of Australia
http://catalogue.nla.gov.au

Printed in Australia by Brougham Press

CONTENTS

AN INVITATION

Cardinal Martini offered the meditations collected in this volume during a retreat he preached to second year theology students at the Saronno Seminary from 11–16 March 1984. He never reviewed the transcript, but this did not prevent it being published by *Edizioni Borla* in 1985. The current re-release seeks to offer the reader the perennial freshness of Martini on a theme which touches crucially on the identity, mission and destiny of communities and the entire Church.

The leading idea is that of *apostolic consciousness*. Martini sets about the task by taking three New Testament passages as his starting point. He demonstrates – through his chosen examples: Jesus in Luke 14, Paul in Acts 13, and Peter in Mark 14 – how such consciousness must go hand in hand with the utmost freedom from judgement by others, and the determination to pursue our journey in the clear-cut awareness of our identity and mission.

The Cardinal clarifies the background and *context* of such apostolic consciousness by referring to Paul. We need to adopt an attitude of listening where God is concerned, since 'the Spirit does not reveal himself in the community and individuals at slack times when they are caught up or involved in a thousand other things. To reveal himself the Spirit asks for recollection' along with 'a degree of bodily austerity' expressed by fasting, 'a discipline of the senses which we need to pay more attention to at specific times.'

Then there is the very *fact* of God manifesting himself: it hinges on my inner readiness to allow myself to be moulded, guided, directed by the action of the Spirit. Prayer is an unmistakable expression of this attitude. Over and above a more simplistic understanding of it, prayer is 'not only praying in view of doing something better' but it 'results in the choice of forming our life, beginning with gospel choices we have internalised,' such that the mission itself becomes 'an integration of gospel values in us according to the divine call.'

There is a true and proper 'baptismal root' of apostolic consciousness, and the archbishop attempts to explain it with reference to 2 Corinthians 4:6: the aim of apostolic life is always that of letting 'light shine out of darkness, who has shone in our hearts to give the light of the knowledge of the glory of God in the face of Jesus Christ.' But there is a darker side we need to guard against, one that risks obscuring our consciousness, sometimes out of laziness, where prayer and discipline are concerned, sometimes due to an insufficient cultural development and lack of 'intellectual conversation', or sometimes due to a subtle hypocrisy or the failure to grasp the central place of the *kerygma*.

All the scriptural examples of mission knew these risks only too well. The list of 'founding' ministries of the community contained in Ephesians 4 recognises in apostles, prophets, evangelists, pastors and teachers (theologians ...), the messengers whose freedom lies uniquely in corresponding faithfully to the mission received. In a certain sense there is a 'passivity of the apostle' which is the guarantee of 'success', not according to the world, but according to the will of God. In fact, the one who is sent 'receives a service whose principal agent is the risen Christ.' And it is clear that 'awareness of ministry as something entrusted to us is the source of a great strength of freedom and peace because it does not have us using a literal measure, which requires immediate success, but God's power as the measure, at work infallibly in history in its own times and ways.'

The very meaning of mission derives from Christ, then, sent by the Father. Martini's concluding meditations are dedicated to Christ, his relationship with the Father and the people to whom he was sent, and to the way he once again bolstered Peter's apostolic consciousness, and reconfirmed Paul's. He concludes with a clarion call of hope, that 'Jesus will comfort our apostolic consciousness at the most difficult moments.' It is up to us to give the Lord times and ways of listening to him which will allow for circumstances in our physical situation in which we can receive the comforting Word.

Giuseppe Mazza

INTRODUCTION

I agreed to preach this retreat to you out of a keen desire for communication in faith, something the bishop also needs. In fact, the bishop lives – as does every Christian – by the Word of God: the Word communicated directly by God and also the Word communicated and spread in the context of the Church.

So I nurture the hope of giving, receiving, and disseminating the Word over these days spent together.

Nevertheless, I feel there is an even deeper motive for which I accepted your invitation and let me put it to you in the words of the Apostle Paul: 'for an obligation is laid on me, and woe to me if I do not proclaim the gospel!' (1 Cor 9:16).

It is a necessity I cannot shirk, especially preaching it to those who are closest to my own journey. It is such a strong need in me that I feel it is a theme to reflect on together with you. Beginning with Paul's exclamation, we should be able to explain the theme this way: mission consciousness, that is, the awareness of being sent.

Paul writes: 'For if I do this of my own will, I have a reward' – it is something that I do, say, that regards me and my profession – 'but if not of my own will, I am entrusted with a commission' (1 Cor 9:17).

This is how it has been for me: in accepting your invitation, I felt a duty given me by Another.

The words of the Apostle which are translated as 'not of my own will' is *ákon* in Greek, or 'not spontaneously'. It is interesting, because we find the opposite term in a passage from the First Letter of Peter: 'tend the flock that is in your charge, exercising the oversight, not under compulsion but *willingly*' (5:2) 'Willingly' or *ekoúsion*, is exactly the opposite of 'not of my own will', *ákon*, which Paul used.

It is this mystery that attracted me, leading me to reflect on what the apostle's consciousness is and thus the consciousness of apostolic vocation or mission in a general sense. What is this consciousness of something I choose, but which is not really my choice in the end, because it is given to me? In fact, I do it out of a duty received and not because of some plan for my life that I myself suggested.

There is another New Testament text which well expresses the strange impression the Apostle feels when he is doing what he wants to do, but at the same time is doing what someone else wants, through him and in him.

We find it in Acts, and it will be the point of reference for our retreat: '*Set apart* for me Barnabas and Saul for the work *to which I have called them*' (13:2). It is the Lord who is setting apart, who is calling.

By mission consciousness, then, I mean the awareness that one is pursuing a project and at the same time obeying a mandate.

I would like to explore this intuition for myself and each of you, in such a way that you can grasp the specific moment of the journey you are experiencing as both choice and mandate.

STARTING WITH YOU

It is important that each individual embarks on these days of retreat by starting out from his own journey and the place where he truly is right now.

Three questions can help you:

(a) What do *I want* from these days? How would I like to come away from them? It is a question which represents 'the ideal', and it can elicit some of the desires you have in your heart.

(b) What do *I expect* from these days? It is a different question from the first one because it concerns the current reality. What am I *actually* expecting as I experience it and as a result of this? Do I expect to be bored, to struggle, or to be content? Am I just looking for moments of tranquillity? Do I expect feelings of peace or am I afraid of prolonged silence and times of struggle?

(c) What sort of temptations and events could *hinder me* from achieving what I want?

It would be wonderful to be able to communicate all this so that the retreat master can manage to follow each of your journeys. Saying 'journey' is different from saying 'consciousness'. Another closely connected word to this is 'conscience', the moral conscience or awareness expressed in sacramental confession. But yet another is the journey made up of a series of inner desires, fears and future anticipation.

Suggestions and fears

(a) Let me offer you a *suggestion* regarding prayer. It could be that prayer suggestions from the biblical texts are a little too broad: they are difficult because the suggestion is made at the level of *lectio* (careful reading) and *meditatio* (meditation), that is, by extending the text in its internal structure and relationship.

It is one thing for something to be suggested, and quite another for each individual to carry it out. So you should not be anxious about picking up on all the things you hear or note. Instead, it is important for you to calmly stay with what leads to *contemplatio,* or contemplation.

Each of you can gradually learn to discern between the many things needed for your education, including your spiritual education, and the things you need to select for your own profound inner nourishment.

(b) I always feel some *trepidation* when I begin preaching a retreat. I fear the effort needed to communicate faith and I especially fear the words and religious attitudes induced by habit and environment. I also fear my lack of preparation with respect to the Word. So let us speak to the Lord in trust and humility.

Lord, you always spoke according to truth. Help us to speak not according to the commonalities and spontaneous associations of religious language, but with the language of truth. You are infinitely greater than any inability of ours. Grant us your Spirit so that it is he who speaks in us to lead us along authentic paths.

Grant that we may overcome our hesitations, and grant us the purifying silence which cuts through our loose thoughts and probes our consciousness of our call and mission.

Guide us, Jesus, along desert paths and the path of Baptism, because it was precisely at the Jordan, after the temptation, that you became conscious of your mandate.

Mary, mother of authenticity, help us to only speak true, simple words which correspond to truth.

As saintly protectors, let us call on St Charles Borromeo, who acquired consciousness of his mission shortly before his priestly ordination during the Retreat in 1563, and St Paul, who often had recourse in his Letters to apostolic consciousness as one of his solid places of refuge at times of difficulty.

1

APOSTOLIC CONSCIOUSNESS

I would like to introduce you to personal reflection by replying to the question:

– What does apostolic consciousness mean, and as a consequence, what does it mean not to have it or to have it in an immature, imperfect or obscure way?

The answer is suggested to us by three episodes in the New Testament.

Jesus preaches at Nazareth (Lk 4:16-30)

The first episode is Jesus preaching at Nazareth, according to Luke's account. Let us briefly consider the succession of events to understand the structure of the passage and how it highlights Jesus' consciousness of his mission.

Jesus experiences a range of reactions, resistance and opposition, of a kind that put his perception of self very much to the test.

– The first reaction is one of intense, captivated attention: 'The eyes of all in the synagogue were fixed on him' (v. 20). It is almost a magnetic sensation one can have when speaking in public: the crowd seems so interested, smitten to the point of focusing strongly on the person speaking, investing the individual with value to some degree. Jesus experiences this reaction: well then, the people are ready, disposed to hearing an important word from me!

– Nonetheless, this situation deteriorates rapidly: 'All spoke well of him and were amazed at the gracious words that came from his mouth.' It seems there is still admiration and wonder, but suspicion appears immediately after this: 'They said, "Is not this Joseph's son?"' (v. 22). It is difficult to explain the complexity of this verse in psychological terms. Jesus feels he is the object of increasing scrutiny and not too well-disposed scrutiny at that. This happens when someone is addressing others and becomes aware that the earlier and fully favourable disposition changes inexplicably at a certain point to reservation and criticism, creating discomfort in both speaker and listener. It is the painful and difficult sensation of seeing one's words begin to be weighed, judged, perhaps misunderstood, with the possibility they could even be used against the speaker.

– After Jesus' strong reaction to this, suspicious astonishment turns hostile and becomes rejection:

> When they heard this, all in the synagogue were filled with rage. They got up, drove him out of the town, and led him to the brow of the hill on which their town was built, so that they might hurl him over the cliff (vv. 28-29).

From kindly attention and suspense, we have come to a complete reversal of the situation, even outrage and outright rejection. This takes place in a setting where Jesus was known and had public influence. It would have caused much discomfort for Jesus' acquaintances, his mother and closest relations. It is as if Jesus had brought dishonour to the family name and been the cause of a sudden uprising among the people: we don't like you, we couldn't care less what you say; mind your own business, go somewhere else, we don't want to listen to you, you have disgraced yourself.

– How does it end? 'But he passed through the midst of them and went on his way.' (v. 30). I interpret Jesus' apostolic consciousness in this mysterious phrase 'he passed through the midst of them.'

The people, who had been caught up in a moment of popular fury, might have quickly understood that it was going overboard to treat him this way, to throw him off the cliff. Perhaps they hesitated, wavered. Jesus, fully aware of himself, regains control of the situation and moves on. 'He went down to Capernaum, a city in Galilee, and was teaching them on the sabbath' (v. 31).

Faced with this apostolic consciousness of Jesus, we can ask ourselves how we might have reacted in his place. I believe it is easy to imagine it. Firstly, great anxiety as the crowd begin whispering, then inner seething rage, anger and quite probably, depression: I am not capable, I can't do this, the mission is too much for me, I've been too presumptuous, it would be best for me to pull out and let someone else do it.

This is a deficient or uncertain apostolic consciousness, one measured by the response from others. When the response is outstandingly positive, we swell with pride and everything goes well, but when the response is negative, we are fearful and hide our anxiety and doubts.

Jesus is the model of apostolic consciousness because he continues straight on as if nothing had happened, and picks up again elsewhere with his patient, orderly preaching of the Word.

Paul and the pagan world (Acts 13:4-12)

The second episode describes for us Paul's confrontation with the pagan world after the beginning of his mission. Paul and Barnabas had gone down to Seleucia and from there had gone to Cyprus where they were proclaiming God's Word:

When they had gone through the whole island as far as Paphor, they met a certain magician, a Jewish false prophet, named Bar-Jesus. He was with the pro-consul, Sergius Paulus, an intelligent man, who summoned Barnabas and wanted to hear the Word of God. But the magician Elymas (for that is the translation of his name) opposed them and tried to turn the pro-consul away from the faith (vv. 6-8).

On the one hand the situation is positive: the pro-consul is an intelligent and prudent man, and called Barnabas and Paul to him, thus opening an important door to evangelisation for them. On the other hand, there is Elymas, the pro-consul's friend and adviser, who wields authority because he is a magician (in the then world, whoever had occult powers was well-considered and revered). Sergius Paulus, a Gentile, is certainly influenced by the magician, who is also a prophet with the gift of the gab, and knows how to proclaim serious matters. We know of magical, obscure writings of the time or shortly thereafter, for example the words of Hermetes Trismegisto: they are works full of grandiose words, mysterious though somewhat opaque concepts, but able to make a great impression. This Elymas, unfortunately for Barnabas and Paul, also bore the name Bar-Jesus, so he was able to exploit an aura of mystery linked to the person of Jesus.

To interfere in the bond of friendship between the magician and the pro-consul was risky.

We would probably have steered clear, said something to the pro-consul, so as not to make an enemy of him, but without directly confronting the situation.

Instead, Paul launches into some dangerous invective that could ruin everything, and put an end to any preaching. He risked their being expelled from the island:

> But Saul, also known as Paul, filled with the Holy Spirit, looked intently at him and said, 'You son of the devil, you enemy of all righteousness, full of all deceit and villainy, will you not stop making crooked the straight paths of the Lord? And now listen – the hand of the Lord is against you, and you will be blind for a while, unable to see the sun' (vv. 9-11).

Behind these words we can read a profound awareness of his mission. Only a man at peace, inwardly secure, and moved by the Spirit, who has understood the power of Jesus' mission and that this was the moment to stand up and show who he was, could speak this way.

Paul's apostolic consciousness leads to clear, transparent, determined and precise actions. On the contrary, a lack of such perception becomes the source of hesitancy and instability, making all of a person's actions uncertain and compromised. St Jerome describes the situation thus: '[Whoever makes a request] does so with faith, without hesitation, because whoever hesitates is like a wave tossed and stirred up by the wind; for the doubter being double-minded and unstable in every way must not expect to receive anything from the Lord' (Jas 1:6-7).

Peter's fall (Mk 14:16-72)

After the models of Jesus' and Paul's apostolic consciousness, we can reflect on the figure of Peter, who in a certain sense represents our situation of immature and uncertain apostolic consciousness.

Let us begin with some verses from Mark's Gospel which are characteristic of Peter's road to denial:

> And Jesus said to them, 'You will all become deserters: for it is written, "I will strike the shepherd, and the sheep will be scattered." But after I am raised up, I will go before you to Galilee.' Peter said to him, 'Even though all become deserters, I will not.' Jesus said to him, 'Truly, I tell you, this day, this very night, before the cock crows thrice, you will deny me three times.' But he said vehemently, 'Even though I must die with you, I will not deny you' (Mk 14:27-31).

Peter apparently has a strong apostolic and mission consciousness, feels sure of himself, but an unsure heart corresponds to these words: they are sincerely uttered but nonetheless untrue. We too can often be sincere, that is, we can express how things are, superficially, in the here and now, but we are not truthful, we do not express what we are thinking deep down. Being authentic means being 'autós', ourselves, fully ourselves; we are halfway to ourselves and what we say is not the truth of our self.

So, Peter is sincere, but not truthful. He has a vacillating, uncertain apostolic awareness but does not know it.

This uncertain awareness is very soon proven when Jesus says, in the Garden of Gethsemane: 'Simon, are you asleep?

Could you not keep awake one hour?' (v. 37). Why could Peter not stay awake for just one hour? Why are we unable to stay awake in certain situations, while at other times we succeed perfectly? We give in to sleep, fatigue, boredom when we are not convinced we have to do what we are doing, or we find it unpleasant and are not sure it is important. On the contrary, when we believe it is important, very useful, then we don't feel tired and the body is ready, our strengths are mobilised by the certainty of action. Jesus invites Peter to pray and Peter understands neither the gravity of the hour nor Jesus' command. He is inwardly uncertain, does not feel that praying at that moment is important for him, so his strengths are not mobilised. Thus, Peter yields to sleep. It is the first sign of his wavering; the second follows on:

'All of them deserted him and fled' (v. 50).

All of them, Peter included, had lost any meaningful reason for having to remain there. If Jesus is handing himself over, if he is showing himself to be so weak, who is obliging us to remain? Why should we? In whose name, by what authority and to achieve what end? Very quickly, mission consciousness falls apart.

Finally, there is Peter's denial (vv. 66-72). Peter is floundering, unable to control himself and behaves other than he would like to; he would like to stay close by Jesus, but is afraid to present himself openly. He falls.

Peter's fall is the consequence of wavering, inner uncertainty, not knowing up to what point he should follow Jesus, how much he should risk. Peter has lost the sense of mission and the clear awareness of why he has been called.

For personal reflection

I simply wanted to introduce you to reflection on apostolic consciousness. For your personal work, I suggest two possibilities:

– Reflect on these episodes, comparing them with your own life and asking yourself: Where do I find signs in me of mature awareness like that of Jesus and Paul? And where, instead, do I find signs in me of immature, uncertain, vacillating awareness, of struggling progress? Why are there such signs?

– Or, take the episodes, read them again, gain deeper understanding of them, pray about them, compare yourself to them, find other episodes in the New Testament and the Scriptures where there seems to be a clear or uncertain consciousness of mission.

Let us ask the Lord to help us begin this journey of deeper understanding and quest:

Lord Jesus, we contemplate the calm you experienced at Nazareth in your first act of preaching. We contemplate the distress you certainly suffered seeing the people's rebellion. You loved them and knew their weakness and wretchedness. You neither allowed yourself to become petty nor did you repulse them or feel self-disgust.

Lord Jesus, we thank you because your consciousness of mission is so great. Grant that ours may be bolstered by yours. Amen.

2

THE ROOTS OF APOSTOLIC CONSCIOUSNESS

Lord Jesus, make firm our steps and guide us along the journey we wish to take. Reassure our hearts and open them up to your Word, dispelling whatever there is in us which could hinder our simple attention to it.

Mary, Mother of the Lord, you attended to this Word at length, affirmed and accompanied its early expression in the Church. Grant that we may adopt a listening attitude to your Son so we may be capable of speaking words that express your truth.

We could meditate on the deep roots of Paul's apostolic consciousness in Acts 9:5-6, where the story of his conversion is recounted, then his encounter with Ananias, who baptised him (9:10-18). While his initial encounter with Christ on the road to Damascus is the absolute and decisive point of departure, it is the episode in Acts 13 where his consciousness assumes its most mature ecclesial dimension:

> Now in the church at Antioch there were prophets and teachers: Barnabas, Simeon who was called Niger, Lucius of Cyrene, Manaen a member of the court of Herod the ruler, and Saul. While they were

worshipping the Lord and fasting, the Holy Spirit said, 'Set apart for me Barnabas and Saul for the work to which I have called them.' Then after fasting and praying, they laid their hands on them and sent them off (vv. 1-3).

The context of Acts 13

'Now in the church at Antioch....': these words give us a context and an action which completely shape the Apostle's consciousness.

It is a threefold *context*: a community, a community at prayer, a fasting community.

(a) *The community*. The background is the Antioch community, and the Greek text is more eloquent: 'Now in Antioch, in the church that was underway there ...' The context of local church, then, is much more precise and detailed than the context of Paul's call and conversion in Chapter 9. There, Paul's personal encounter with Jesus is described, along with his being sent on to a disciple, Ananias, a man of great prudence who is well-considered in the local scene: there is no further specification of any relationship with a community. Ananias fulfils what is almost the role of a spiritual director, who verifies then brings Paul's conversion to completion.

Instead, in Chapter 13 we are clearly in an ecclesial community context: a fervent, lively church with prophets and teachers, as we learn from additional information furnished by the text. We are not simply faced with a tiny handful of disciples as we might assume is the case with Ananias. This church in Antioch has first-order functions.

The *prophets* are authoritative proclaimers, interpreters whose task is to make the Word relevant: with charismatic authority – recognised, hence, with ecclesial authority – they proclaim the Word of God in its significance for people today. They are valuable and essential, especially in the context of a living church. We do not really have an equivalent term today but might call them preachers or great present-day witnesses.

The *teachers* explore, explain and organise a visible body of expression, cues from the Word, placing all this in relationship with the living situation and historical journey of the community. These would correspond to our theologians today.

Other charisms are not indicated in this passage and what follows in the account makes us think that the omission of the evangeliser is not completely by accident. The evangeliser is one of the founding charisms of the Church. In Ephesians 4, mention is made of the five great charisms which make up the ecclesial community: apostles, prophets, evangelists, pastors, teachers. The evangeliser is probably not named here because it is still an evolving role: among these men are some who will be called to evangelise. We can take from this that not all the charisms shine out in a community. Some emerge at one time, others at another, and new ones arise too. It is true that every charism is needed, but not all are exercised in an evident and radiant way, and it is really this fact that makes the history of individual communities different.

Who are the prophets and teachers in Acts 13?

Barnabas: a generous individual who made a gesture of great evangelical poverty at the outset, stripping himself of his belongings on behalf of the poor in the community.

Simeon: nicknamed Niger, perhaps because he came from Africa. He brings us a different culture.

Lucius of Cyrene: probably bound up with the Hellenist movement, like the synagogue at Cyrene, spoken of in reference to Stephen.

Hanaen: a childhood friend of Herod the Tetrarch; a man prepared for court work, with personal skills in doing and speaking.

These are all committed lay people who come from the world of civil and social responsibilities and who have then made themselves available to the community. We could call it a cosmopolitan, spirited community, pluralist in expression.

(b) *Community at prayer.* This community is celebrating worship of the Lord, and in particular individuals who are named and who perhaps make up a kind of pastoral council or executive body of the community at prayer. The expression 'while they were worshipping the Lord' is fairly rare and taken from the pagan and civil religious world; *leitourgoùnton:* they were 'doing' liturgy.

(c) *A fasting community.* The note is an interesting one: 'and fasting.' What were the elements of this liturgy? The Lord's Supper perhaps? It is possible, but the context is a wider one, a context of silence, listening, common reflection on the Word, fasting.

We could call it a Lenten moment, a retreat.

What does the context tell us? That the Spirit does not reveal himself in communities and individuals at slack times when they are caught up or involved in a thousand other things. To reveal himself, the Spirit asks for recollection, asks the community for days of retreat, and fasting suggests a degree of bodily austerity, a discipline of the senses which we need to pay more attention to at specific times.

The action

A fact, an action, is presented in the context we have tried to describe.

(a) *The actor*, the agent of this deed, is an unusual one: 'the *Holy Spirit* said.' The Holy Spirit of God, God himself, is brought into the action, the supreme instance beyond which there is no higher recourse: it is he who codifies and orders human existence in a final way without possibility of appeal.

The expression finds an echo in Acts 10:19: Peter was on the roof at Simon the tanner's house. He was also at prayer and fasting and had a vision while he was anxiously reflecting on its meaning: 'the Spirit said to him … '

So, we can place two of the Spirit's initiatives for evangelisation in parallel. The Spirit is the commissioner, agent, fundamental actor in evangelising work.

At the beginning of Paul's apostolic journeys – Acts 13 is in fact the introduction to the second part of the Book and hence to Paul's journeys – what is strongly underscored is that once again it is Jesus Christ manifesting himself divinely to his Church through the power of the Spirit.

(b) *How does the Spirit show up?* It is described by the words 'The Holy Spirit said.' By analogy with other similar cases we can consider that we are not dealing with a voice from heaven: rather is it a voice spoken by the Spirit *through an authoritative member of the community.* The mission comes from the Spirit, but is expressed in words; in words that are so authoritative as to be spoken in his name. it does not say: 'The Spirit says to set apart' but is said in first person: 'Set apart *for me.*' The Word is the means, *in* and *of* the Church;

however, it is a Word which the Spirit takes responsibility for. That is, the Spirit takes upon himself the first and immediate responsibility for evangelising work.

What comes to mind is the conclusion the Church makes in the Jerusalem reflection: 'For it has seemed good to the Holy Spirit and to us' (Acts 15:28). It is an expression that emphasises the spiritual consciousness the Church has of itself, of its strict connection with the work of the Spirit.

(c) What is *the result of the Spirit's action*? 'Set apart for me Barnabas and Saul for the work to which I have called them.'

1. The phrase 'set apart' – in Greek the verb *aphorísate* – is important. We find it in the parable-like description of the final judgement in Matthew's Gospel:

> All the nations will be gathered before him and he
> will separate people one from another as a shepherd
> separates the sheep from the goats (Mt 25:32).

It is an action that *chooses, distributes,* sets some, rather than others, *apart*, a real action of power by the Spirit over the human being. Naturally the human being must be ready to accept this power; the liturgy which the Antioch community celebrated is the expression, in prayer, of availability to the *Kyrios*, the Lord Jesus. It is a liturgy that can be summed up briefly by the invocation: Lord, take possession of our lives; do with us as you want.

In a manner of speaking, the Spirit assumes management of human industriousness, requests it for himself.

The verb 'set apart' is characteristic of Paul's apostolic and mission consciousness. When he has to describe himself for the community in Rome, who do not know him, he will say:

'Paul, a servant of Jesus Christ, called to be an apostle, set apart [*aphorisménos*] for the gospel of God' (Rom 1:1).

The expression points to the root of Paul's strength: it is not a choice of his, he did not want it, it is not a whim of his; rather it is the Spirit taking possession of his life.

By broadening our reflection, we can think of all those who are living symbols of such action of the Spirit in the lives of individuals: Abraham, Moses, Isaiah, Jeremiah.

2. 'Set apart for me *Barnabas and Saul*.' Barnabas is named first to respect the order according to which he is one of the pillars making up the link with the community in Jerusalem, with the first events, with the Church's tradition.

Saul is named next, even though very soon he will emerge to a point where they come to disagreement. Saul has come from a long period of silence and resentment: his first apostolic attempt went badly for him. He was sent away and certainly felt abandoned. So it is with some trepidation that he returns to a scene of shared responsibility, introduced by Barnabas.

We can easily imagine the stir of surprise among this group of men praying. There were certainly better known, more visible men with more prestige than Paul. The Spirit's intervention, then, has a note of novelty to it, as if to indicate his sovereign freedom to choose.

(3) *'For the work to which I have called them.'* Their being set apart is for an activity, a particular service from on high. The sentence is very brief and looks like a tautology. It actually aims at expressing very clearly that the work is not Paul's, but belongs to the one who calls him and determines the activity. This concept returns immediately afterwards: 'So, being sent

out by the Holy Spirit, they went down to Seleucia.' Everything Paul will do – on this journey, in Asia Minor, then in Europe, and again in Jerusalem while in prison – is conditioned by this very strong sense of call and mission.

When Paul returns to Antioch it will be said that '...they sailed back to Antioch, where they had been commended to the grace of God for the work that they had completed' (14-26). The undertaking – *érgon* – which Paul had been called to, is carried out by the grace of the Lord: it is another way of expressing the powerful mercy of God at work in this service. The community had confirmed and entrusted them, so to speak, to this grace.

Reflections for ourselves

1. Bearing in mind some elements of the *Context* we have explained, we can ask ourselves:

– How do we experience the context in which consciousness of mission is expressed? Is our perspective ecclesial, local Church, diocesan? Is it a context of prayer, liturgy, worship of God? Is it a context of fasting, simplicity, a spirit of renunciation?

– Within the perspective of Church experience, do I know how to grasp awareness of my mission beyond the things that please or do not please me, beyond the daily routine? Do I understand that the journey of the Church I am making is not in view of a successful outcome but of apostolic consciousness to be acquired, and that it presumes a gradual formation?

2. And, on some elements of the 'action' we can ask ourselves:

– Do I know how to grasp this 'action' of apostolic consciousness, of being called, set apart for a service that marks my whole manner of life? This is clearly not some invasion from outside: it is an inspiration of the Holy Spirit, the Spirit giving shape to my life.

I can add a further consideration. It is true that Paul's experience as described in Acts 13:2 is felt intimately at the moment of his mandate. Nonetheless, it is anticipated in us as our baptismal awareness gradually clarifies to become an awareness of being available for a mandate. The absolutely ultimate root of everything that will mature in Paul is the person of Jesus who revealed himself to him on the road to Damascus:

'Who are you, Lord?' And the voice: 'I am Jesus whom you are persecuting' (Acts 9:5). Meanwhile, it makes sense for him to allow himself to be sent on mission by the Spirit, inasmuch as he has recognised the primacy of Jesus in his life: 'But get up and enter the city and you will be told what you are to do' (v. 6). Here, Paul's availability for a mission is already understood and intimated. So, Acts 13:2 indicates the end point of arrival, while Acts 9:5 indicates its baptismal root of conversion, encounter with Christ, which gradually develops and in its successive apostolic experiments becomes full availability to accepting the mandate. Awareness of the mandate presumes a profound baptismal awareness. Before the mission at Antioch, Paul was already working in the Church but in his own name. Following this, he would be in crisis, needing to reflect, having withdrawn from public life for many years before being officially called by the Church.

The journey toward full maturity of mission is long, arduous, demanding, but we cannot shirk it.

3

DISCERNMENT IN APOSTOLIC CONSCIOUSNESS

By reflecting on the context in which Paul achieved the fullness of apostolic consciousness, we have stressed the fact that the community 'were worshipping the Lord' (Acts 13:2).

Today we would like to meditate on this activity of prayer and attentiveness to the Word, in order to understand its relationship with apostolic consciousness.

By way of introduction, let us try to describe a certain simplistic notion of prayer, so we can then open ourselves to a more dynamic one: prayer which moves toward discernment and life.

Christian prayer – its stages

The simplistic notion of prayer can be expressed thus: I would like to undertake something. I see that a certain kind of behaviour would be important and I pray that I may have the grace I need for it. Prayer here is seen as a support, an aid, something that reinforces decisions we claim are already clear and evident.

This kind of prayer is good when certain decisions are already clearly discernible from the context. But it shows its inadequacy when we are dealing with life decisions, choices we must put into action to respond to God's call.

So it is important to reflect on the value of prayer for discernment, on the relationship between prayer and life, and the steps by which prayer enters life and becomes part of it.

The following stages of prayer are well known and can be expressed in a handful of small steps which I will extend to seven, so they can be more useful: *lectio, meditatio, contemplatio, consolatio, discretio, deliberatio, actio.* Their sequence expresses very well the dynamic of prayer as a way of discernment.

(a) *Lectio.* *Lectio* places this prayer in relationship with the Scriptures, because it is a divine reading or *lectio divina.* It consists of reading or listening to a passage from the Bible, seeking to highlight its pivotal elements. It is a dynamic approach, the effort to grasp what stands out in the text in such a way that the 'plain' becomes a 'mountain panorama', some parts lit up, others in the shade. By underlining verbs, subjects, objects, the various elements take on unexpected value. In the framework we are considering it from, *lectio* is not an end in itself but opens up to *meditatio*: it needs to be done each time, so we can have something to take us on from there; not so little that *meditatio* is barren, and not too much that it would only hinder the process.

(b) *Meditatio.* This is reflection on the values in the text, especially perennial values. This is a second way of approaching the passage: no longer thinking analytically about subjects, objects, symbols, inner and outer movements, but values the text is channelling and bringing with it.

Meditatio needs to be done with the mind and also the emotions, because often the values are crammed with interests and feelings. This implies that quality prevails over quantity at this stage, that outward forms, be they geometric figures or syntactic details, give way to their content. This is an important step. What values is Jesus expressing by being this way? What values is Paul expressing and how do I make them my own? The world of *meditatio* is quite varied, because we are comparing ourselves with the Word and making it a model, a resolution, a rule of life. Nevertheless, there is a risk, and it is that of prolonging the exercise *ad infinitum*, luxuriating in having understood the values of the text, put them into some sort of order, and linked them to our own life. The risk is in believing we are living these values simply because we have done well in grasping them. This blocks the dynamic process of prayer and we fall into self-satisfaction which is really the opposite of the evangelical religious spirit, even though it is nurtured by words from the Gospel.

Meditatio, then, is of immense value for us to learn and maybe it takes years to do so. But at some point, it must also be transcended to become *contemplatio*. *Meditatio* can be achieved, to some extent, even by a non-believer who is satisfied with some of the profound values found in Scripture.

(c) *Contemplatio* means entering into the specific Christian prayer which is 'in spirit and truth'. It is the movement from consideration of values to adoration of the person of Jesus who sums up all the values, encapsulates them, expresses them in himself and reveals them. It is a moment of prayer *par excellence* when the very things that were most useful for stimulating our awareness are now forgotten. Jesus is loved and adored, we offer ourselves to him, ask for forgiveness, praise God's greatness, intercede on behalf of our own poverty, or the for world, other people, the Church. The centre and reference point of *contemplatio* is always the person of Jesus who reveals the Father.

From a more properly ontological or supernatural anthropological viewpoint, *contemplatio* is our availability for the infused gift of charity. This means that the human person is in the ideal situation for consciously accepting, or at least being fully ready to accept, the infused gift of charity, allowing the Spirit of holiness to quiver within us.

Contemplatio, then, is partly an active, adoring, loving exercise, and partly a passive one; it is room given to the spirit of Christ for him to adore, praise, glorify the Father in us. The infused gift of charity is present in seminal form, as we know, in every baptised individual. Very often, however, it has no room to express itself, that is, no bodily, mental, structural room. *Contemplatio* is precisely the moment when we provide bodily space for the Holy Spirit. This is why we can also call it 'conversion' as we give ourselves completely to God, choose God constantly and are drawn to him, to love him with our whole heart, mind and all the supernaturally eminent strength we receive from the Holy Spirit.

It is truly the culminating point of the various steps of prayer and is the norm, the reference point for the earlier stages. Insofar as *lectio* is useful, and *meditatio* important, they lead to *contemplatio* which is life in its full sense: the life of Christ alive in the one who is contemplating.

At this point in the dynamics of prayer, we should add that there should be only the infused mystical experience, the conscious perception of God at work. But union with God at mystical levels is not necessarily part of the ordinary setup of Christian life. Instead, I would like to say something to explain the inner dynamics of *contemplatio*, which is why I have indicated a further four steps even though they are not at a level beyond contemplatio, since everything has already happened.

(d) *Consolatio.* We struggle to define this word, yet it is something very well known in the New Testament. Paul makes considerable use of it both as a verb – *parakaléo* – and as a noun – *paráklesi*. He even foresees it as a ministry: 'We have gifts that differ…the exhorter (*paraklón)* in exhortation (*paraklései)*' (Rom 12:6-8). Consolation is one of God's names, the God of patience and consolation (cf. Rom 15:4; 2 Cor 1:3) and the New Testament considers it to be one of the fundamental realities of the Christian experience.

We tend to think of it as a supportive adjunct: the need to be consoled looks to us like a sign of weakness and this is somewhat strange if we consider that the Holy Spirit is presented as the Paraclete, the Consoler.

So what can we mean by *consolatio* as the ordinary development of *contemplatio*? We mean the deep intimate joy that comes from union with God, the radiant, joyful reflection of communion with him.

We think of the joy we see shine through the eyes of particularly holy people, their peace, serenity, tranquillity, even in suffering. This is how they savour worship of God, relationship with God, all experienced with joy.

The person who has arrived at contemplation knows that no human power will be able to strip him or her of the peace that is God's gift. Paul expresses this joyful certainty when he exclaims:

Who will separate us from the love of Christ? Will hardship, or distress, or persecution or famine, or nakedness, or peril, or sword? … For I am convinced that neither death, nor life, nor angels, nor rulers, nor things present, nor things to come, nor powers, nor height, nor depth, nor anything else in all creation will be able to separate us from the love of God in Christ Jesus Our Lord (Rom 8:35, 38-9).

Consolation is the power we feel emanating from Paul's words still, two thousand years later. Consolation has many other names; at certain times in the history of spirituality it has been called 'fervour' or 'devotion' (St Francis de Sales), that is, the joyful and spontaneous readiness with which people give themselves to God. St John Eudes called it 'the kingdom of Jesus': the life and kingdom of Jesus developing in us.

We should not overlook *consolatio*, then. At times a certain pseudo-spiritual culture would have us believe that what counts is to do our duty, be loyal and upright. Yet the loyal and upright person can only but express the fullness of self which is the strength and enthusiasm of inner joy!

For sure we are dealing with deeply hidden spiritual joy. Though it is often veiled and obscured by trials, dryness, desolation, temptation, dereliction, by the cross, the human being is not called to all that. The point the human being is called to is the radiance of the risen Christ across all our experience. It is no mere appendix but something to be distinguished from pure states of natural enthusiasm.

(e) *Discretio* or discernment. *Consolatio* places us in marvellous harmony with gospel values. It is the inner savouring of Christ, of being with him, his poverty, with people who are like Jesus in suffering, of generously following the cross with him. Christ's great choices, his abandonment to the Father, his detachment, dedication to humanity – these all become shared values at the moment of *consolatio*.

Discernment is the ability to choose through an inner, shared nature, according to Christ and as Christ would. Its relationship with *meditatio* is a strict one because *meditatio* brings out Jesus' values and *discretio* has us choose them. Francis of Assisi encounters the leper, sees Christ in him and, under the impulse of the Spirit, kisses him joyfully, overcoming strong natural repugnance: this is the *discretio* that has him make the same choice Jesus makes.

(f) *Deliberatio* is the inner decision one makes for Christ-like choices and it necessarily flows into *actio*.

(g) *Actio*, then, is our way of living and acting according to the Spirit of Christ. It is our total inner acceptance of apostolic consciousness integrated within us. *Actio* is the choice made not just as an act of will which we might struggle to conform to, but a reality within us through the energy of prayer.

This kind of prayer is no longer praying only in view of doing something better: this prayer elicits choice and shapes our life with gospel choices we have internalised. Thus apostolic consciousness becomes the integration of gospel values in us according to the divine call.

The importance of contemplation

Before concluding, I would like to insist on the importance of contemplation without which everything becomes insipid, the arduous execution of precepts, acting moralistically or instinctively. Lack of contemplation hinders us from an overall grasp of the Christian experience and from truly living Jesus' 'Come, follow me.' In contemplation, the person achieves the maximum of clarity and strength, the human project is controlled and continues to be controlled gradually as our contemplative approach is integrated with our actions, culture, and outward expression.

The movement from meditation to contemplation is a vital and decisive one in the Christian experience. Often our Christian experience is at best some nice thoughts at the meditative, reflective level, but still vague regarding many of the values of God's gift to humankind. This is often the apostles' experience in Mark's Gospel, seeing but not understanding, having eyes but not seeing. It leads to uncertainty, struggling with constant rethinking and the desire to evade things, since we do not have contemplation for reference.

The question we can pose for ourselves, then, should be how we practise *lectio* and *meditatio,* but especially whether we are open to contemplation, and consider it fundamental to our faith journey.

I believe we have all had some moments of true contemplation, where we have also been able to discern God's consolation.

The invitation is for you to reflect on these moments and give them their appropriate value according to the Lord's intentions.

4

PAUL'S APOSTOLIC CONSCIOUSNESS

To explore Paul's apostolic consciousness further, as a model and point of reference for our own, let us now try to be enlightened by some autobiographical insights the apostle offers as he is spurred on by argument and opposition.

It also happens to us that we are able to clarify our motives for ourselves, why we do what we do as a result of opposition or our way of acting being questioned.

This happens to Paul. We see it in his Second Letter to the Corinthians. It is an extremely personal argumentative letter in which the Apostle defends himself from the accusations of his enemies, and not just his enemies; he defends himself from misunderstandings and is often forced to appeal to his deeper consciousness.

Our reflection will have two stages: first of all, I will simply offer you some texts found in the early chapters of 2 Corinthians, pointing out their basic significance and recurring patterns. In the following meditation, instead, we will do a *lectio divina* on one of these texts which seems particularly significant to me and sums up what Paul feels about his apostolic consciousness. As personal work, I suggest a continuous reading of the first seven chapters of the same Letter, alongside Acts 13 and some chapters that follow.

Texts from 2 Corinthians

The texts I have garnered from the Letter could also be called texts of 'apostolic investiture', because Paul is reflecting on God's call and does so in different ways and terms.

2 Corinthians 1:21-22: 'But it is God who establishes us with you in Christ and has anointed us, by putting his seal on us and giving us his spirit in our hearts as a first instalment.'

It is not true that Paul did not keep his word as some have suggested. When Paul expresses an intention and tenaciously seeks to make it happen, his firmness is not based on his strength or opinions but on God: it is He who confirms him. The root of his firmness, his sincerity, his truth, lies in what God has made of him.

2 Corinthians 2:17: 'For we are not peddlers of God's word like so many; but in Christ, we speak as persons of sincerity, as persons sent from God and standing in his presence.'

Paul distances himself from other ways of being an apostle, as a peddler or manipulator of the Word who uses it for gain, prestige, and in service of an ideology. Instead, he feels that his words come to him from someone else and he is moved by God to speak. The Greek text says simply: 'With sincerity and from God.' The expression recalls the prophets who spoke 'from God.' (2 Pt 1:21)

2 Corinthians 3:4-6: 'Such is the confidence that we have through Christ toward God. Not that we are competent of ourselves to claim anything, as coming from us; our competence is from God, who has made us competent to be ministers of a new covenant, not of letter but of Spirit: for the letter kills but the Spirit gives life.'

Here, it is not so much the Apostle's way of acting that is justified and clarified, but his feelings and confidence. The people see that he is a secure person, profoundly self-assured. In fact, it is God who has made him a minister suited to the Covenant of the Spirit.

2 Corinthians 4:1-2: 'Therefore, since it is by God's mercy that we are engaged in this ministry we do not lose heart. We have renounced the shameful things that one hides; we refuse to practise cunning or to falsify God's word; but by the open statement of the truth we commend ourselves to the conscience of everyone in the sight of God.'

Faced with discouragement, a sense of defeat that could result from opposition to the Word, Paul refers to the clarity and sincerity with which he speaks before God. God sent him, told him what to say, and he carried out the divine mandate in all confidence and tranquillity, without concern for the consequences. His approach is not deceptive; he proclaims the Word as it is, in the awareness of being sent by God and giving glory and honour to Him alone.

2 Corinthians 4:5-6: 'For we do not proclaim ourselves; we proclaim Jesus Christ as Lord and ourselves as your slaves for Jesus' sake. For it is the God who said, 'Let light shine out of darkness' who has shone in our hearts to give the light of the knowledge of the glory of God in the face of Jesus Christ.'

I do not preach myself. I preach Christ and it is God himself who has placed me in this light which I use to enlighten others.

2 Corinthians 4:7-11: But we have this treasure in clay jars, so that it may be made clear that this extraordinary power belongs to God and does not come from us. We are afflicted in every way, but not crushed; perplexed, but not driven to despair; persecuted, but not forsaken; struck down, but not destroyed; always carrying in the body the death of Jesus, so that the life of Jesus may also be made visible in our bodies. For while we live we are always being given up to death for Jesus' sake, so that the life of Jesus may be made visible in our mortal flesh.'

This passage is known as 'the apostolic paradox'. Paul compares his outward situation (the 'Paul phenomenon' as people who did not know Christ saw him) to the inner reality he experiences. The outward phenomenon is the jar of clay: fragility, weakness, fatigue, tiredness, but all this is because it seems that his extraordinary strength comes from God. It is the confession of the twin experience of weakness and strength. Paul's apostolic consciousness is not triumphal: on the contrary, it is suffering, labouring, troubled, anxious but just the same, God's strength penetrates it in a powerful way.

2 Corinthians 4:13-14: 'But just as we have the same spirit of faith that is in accordance with scripture – 'I believed, and so I spoke' – we also believe, and so we speak, because we know that the one who raised the Lord Jesus will raise us also with Jesus and will bring us with you into his presence.'

This is the reminder of the roots of faith. God gives us faith and then we say with conviction that the victory is already his: as he triumphed in Christ so will he also triumph in us.

2 Corinthians 4:16: 'So we do not lose heart. Even though our outer nature is wasting away, our inner nature is being renewed day by day.'

He resumes his psychological conviction that could be disputed by the fact that he is not only fragile but getting older, more tired, more irritable, more inclined to depression. Nevertheless, he has learned to distinguish between what he *feels* in terms of immediate sensitivity, *and what is really happening to him* deep within. He has come to the point of discernment which grasps hold of consolation as something deeply felt, even amid the annoyance and outward unrest of his feelings.

2 Corinthians 5:5: 'He who has prepared us for this very thing is God, who has given us the Spirit as a guarantee.'

The root of everything is God: the ongoing current proof of this is the guarantee of the Spirit.

2 Corinthians 5:11: 'Therefore, knowing the fear of the Lord, we try to persuade others; but we ourselves are well known to God, and I hope that we are also well known to your consciences.'

Here, there is probably also a sense of realism: Paul tries to persuade, but not everyone is persuaded, and indeed some misinterpret his words and attribute other intentions to him. However, God knows him and it is his relationship with God that gives Paul his sense of security.

2 Corinthians 5:13: 'For if we are beside ourselves, it is for God; if we are in our right mind, it is for you.'

The apostle knows that his preaching has occupied him to the point where he is being judged as excessive, someone who demands too much, beyond what is reasonable. But he is doing it for God who calls him irresistibly; and then he adapts to his listeners, tries to understand them, remains close to them in their gradual journey. This kind of awareness, which we often experience in ourselves, seems to me to be very important. We have such great things to say that it could sound like madness to anyone looking on from outside, so we adapt, refrain from saying everything clearly and strongly because it would not be understood. Then we speak in parables, take to the road for a while like Jesus with the disciples from Emmaus, expecting that the revelation will become clear. Paul, then, is speaking in a way prompted by his apostolic consciousness.

2 Corinthians 5:14-15: 'For the love of Christ urges us on, because we are convinced that one has died for all: therefore, all have died. And he died for all, so that those who live might live no longer for themselves but for him who died and was raised for them.'

Christ's love is the root of Paul's apostolic approach, but this love urges everyone on because Christ died for everyone.

2 Corinthians 5:18: 'All this is from God, who reconciled us to himself through Christ and has given us the ministry of reconciliation.'

It was God who reconciled us to himself through Christ and his ministers: the divine origin of ministry is once again stressed.

2 Corinthians 6:1: 'As we work together with him, we urge you also not to accept the grace of God in vain.'

Paul is not acting in first person: it is God who acts and Paul is simply collaborating. This is an interesting expression of apostolic awareness.

---

2 Corinthians 6:4-5: '... but as servants of God we have commended ourselves in every way: through great endurance, in afflictions, hardships, calamities, beatings, imprisonments, riots, labours, sleepless nights, hunger.'

This is no longer a list of paradoxes but of the Apostle's humiliations placed in contrast with what Paul feels he is experiencing by the grace of God: purity, knowledge, kindness etc. This is how Paul describes his way of experiencing all his difficulties in Christ.

General reflections on the texts and recurring patterns

Let us now see about making some general reflections on the fifteen texts I have quoted.

(a) The very abundance of the texts indicates that Paul experienced these things intensely, that his ministry was sustained by a strong awareness of it, and that he had very much internalised his awareness to the extent that he could put it into words. We are clearly faced with an already mature, tried and tested Paul who has been through the fire and water of his ministry, and at the same time, we understand that ministry must be experienced in a crescendo of awareness. If we do not cultivate awareness, at a certain point the motives for why we do things dry up. Therefore we should love the difficulties and adversity that our ministry encounters when it is experienced in its truth. If we experience these things as a test, they will make us grow in awareness of the meaning of what we are about. Easy things, by contrast, lead to laziness and do not help us mature in the meaning of our call.

(b) The texts refer sometimes to Paul's apostolic awareness and at other times to the community's. 'It is God who establishes us with you in Christ and has anointed us' (2 Cor 1:21). This recalls the common roots of ministry: baptism, confirmation, spirit.

Again: 'But just as we have the same spirit of faith ... we also believe, and so we speak' (2 Cor 4:13-14). The faith is the whole community's even if it is especially intense in Paul. They are all rooted in faith and feel the need to speak.

'Even though our outer nature is wasting away, our inner nature is being renewed day by day' (4:16). Paul appeals to a fundamental Christian awareness: the hope of eternal life is for the whole community.

So, we see this interesting phenomenon: the same expression indicates both Paul's and the community's apostolic awareness.

We are called to live out the continuity between the baptismal and the apostolic gift as we have already emphasised, by reflecting on the relationship between Paul's conversion (Acts 9) and his ecclesial call (Acts 13). Ministry is not something that comes totally from without: it is the development of the roots that lie in baptism and confirmation. At a certain point, through a specific call, it takes on the same fullness, breadth, depth it has in Paul and that is bound up with the community's.

Our apostolic, priestly, evangelising call has its roots in the baptismal call of the whole community. We share in this gift with the community and are its privileged expression, not its only one or a separate one. We are leaders and life-givers of the entire Church's missionary charism.

(c) The third reflection can come from an analysis of patterns in the texts. There are various formal patterns that a careful *lectio* enables us to identify and which find correspondence in other patterns of apostolic or mission consciousness in Old or New Testaments.

I can identify *four basic patterns:*

1. *A simple, straightforward pattern*: it expresses the divine root of apostolic consciousness. For example: 'it is God who establishes us with you in Christ' (2 Cor 1:21). This gift is from God. An equally straightforward version of Jesus' consciousness comes to mind: 'I came that they may have life and have it abundantly' (Jn 10:10). Here is Jesus expressing his awareness in an immediate, simple way.

2. *A binary pattern*: with two distinct elements: what God is doing and what God has human beings do. For example: 'For it is the God who said, "Let light shine out of darkness," who has shone in our hearts to give the light of the knowledge of the glory of God' (2 Cor 4:5-6).

The first element is extended in this text: God the Creator, who has illuminated the world. He who made me, called me and shone in me. This probes the meaning of God and as a consequence the meaning of human activity.

3. *A pattern of contrasts* where two behaviours are opposed: this pattern features a 'but'. For example: 'For we are not peddlers of God's word like so many; but in Christ we speak as persons of sincerity ... ' (2 Cor 2:17). The straightforward, direct pattern is simply 'in Christ' or 'sent by God'. Yet it is introduced by a pattern of contrasts: not like ... but like ... Apostolic consciousness is specified by contrasting it with other things. It is a pattern we find in the Gospel where, for

example, Jesus says: 'I have come to call not the righteous but sinners' (Mk 2:17). Not for one thing but for another.

In the first Letter to the Corinthians: 'Christ did not send me to baptise but to proclaim the Gospel' (1 Cor 11:17). A particular awareness of Paul's is even better specified in the field of ministry: the awareness of being made for first proclamation, to proclaim the Gospel, and being called for this before anything else.

4. *A composite or hypothetical pattern,* where there is an 'if' and a 'then'. If this is how things are, then it follows that ... For example: 'For the love of Christ urges us on because we are convinced that one has died for all ...and he died for all...' (2 Cor 5:14-15). There is an 'if' built in here: if, given that Christ died for all, it follows that we no longer live for ourselves, but for him.

'Therefore, since it is by God's mercy that we are engaged in this ministry, we do not lose heart. We have renounced the shameful things ... refused to practise cunning ... but by the open statement of the truth we commend ourselves to the conscience of everyone in the sight of God' (2 Cor 4:1-2). Here the contrasting pattern is introduced by a conditional clause, 'since ... '

We can ask ourselves what value this formal analysis may have other than practising a *lectio,* that is, improving our understanding of the crucial elements of the text.

Its value is in understanding how Paul really expressed his deepest apostolic consciousness in so many ways.

Saying the same thing in a myriad of different ways, in fact indicates that something is firmly rooted in us. I recall a teacher once saying that to have learned something means being able to say it in fifteen different ways without ever repeating yourself!

We have looked at fifteen texts in which Paul expresses the same idea with ever new variation because he has a real, not just a notional understanding of his apostolic awareness.

Reflections for ourselves

Often the apostolic awareness we have of ourselves is similar to the seed without roots in the parable of the sower.

The seed withers when it encounters its first difficulties, since it has not struck deep roots. Opposition, one difficulty after another, some misunderstanding around us and we immediately flounder, waver, vacillate inwardly.

Let us ask the Lord:

Lord, plant the seed of our Christian vocation, our baptism and confirmation, deep within us. Then, on the stem its deep roots have grown, graft and enliven, O Lord, the sense of call and mission. Do not allow minor problems, what friends say, the different mindsets books TV, media, public opinion give us – do not, we say, allow these things to make us waver regarding this fundamental conviction. Strike roots for us in our weakness so that we can say with the Apostle Paul: we are a clay jar but our strength comes from you. You are our life, Lord Jesus!

5

THE BAPTISMAL ROOT OF
APOSTOLIC CONSCIOUSNESS

Lord, it was Jesus who told us that it is the Spirit in us, not we ourselves, who is speaking. Place the words of the Spirit on our lips, so we can express the mystery we bear within and which is your gift.

By meditating on the baptismal root of mission consciousness, we will now seek to develop the *lectio* of one particularly significant text among those we have considered as a group.

A lectio of 2 Corinthians 4:6

The context is in verse 5: 'For we do not proclaim ourselves; we proclaim Jesus Christ as Lord and ourselves as your slaves for Jesus' sake.' Paul then goes on: 'For it is the God who said, 'Let light shine out of darkness' who has shone in our hearts to give the light of the knowledge of the glory of God in the face of Jesus Christ' (v. 6).

Within the one syntactic composition we can understand how rich in thoughts and feelings this passage is. It is a text that allows us to grasp it as being the baptismal root for Paul because, as in the others already quoted, he refers it to himself as justification for the fact that he preaches Jesus, not himself. He refers initiative in his life to God: the initiative of his baptism (Acts 9) and his apostolic initiative (Acts 13).

By 'baptismal root' we clearly do not only mean baptism as a sacrament, separate from the rest of our existence, because then we would be referring to our time as an infant. By 'baptism' we mean the sacrament of conversion which reaches its fullness when adults accept Christ as the Lord of their life.

This growth is a gradual one. Certainly, there are precocious spiritual moments when even at a very young age there can be the deep intuition of Christ the Lord, the absoluteness of God in a person's life. Ordinarily, however, this consciousness grows gradually with human maturing and achieves more responsible and consistent terms at the time of First Communion, Confirmation. But a true acceptance of Christ probably does not take place before 18–20 years of age, when one is faced with determining choices which involve this perception. It is only toward 30–40 years of age, according to some psychologists, that integration of the Lordship of Christ occurs within the whole person and his or her sentiments. Then, in practical terms, it continues throughout life. So, the baptismal root is there in us from the moment of our baptism, but it is as part of a journey that it is integrated within the historical complexities of our existence.

The text of 2 Corinthians 4:6 is a valid paradigm for us all; of our baptismal roots and our apostolic awareness.

Let us divide it into three parts:

– God's action: '… the God who said, 'Let light shine out of darkness';

– The action as received by Paul: 'shone in our hearts';

– The action in its ministerial effect; 'to give the light of the knowledge of the glory of God in the face of Jesus Christ.'

1. God's action

- '... the God who said, "Let light shine out of darkness."' Paul wants to tie this sentence directly to the one that follows, 'shone in our hearts,' to indicate that it is God himself. Of themselves the two sentences could be expressed by combining them, but the Apostle wants the strong link to stand out between God's action and God's action in him.

Who is this God of whom Paul is speaking? Not some generic divinity but the Father – *ho Théos* – understood as the Absolute, the beginning of everything, the origin, the ultimate, the one who conditions everything and is conditioned by nothing, the Father of Jesus Christ. This is the very origin, in the divine milieu, of the One and only God, God's unity, the root of roots, the light from which all light comes.

– *'who said'* – *ho eipón* – he who spoke. It is interesting that since Paul is talking about God as the creative and absolute origin of everything, the one beyond whom nothing can be thought to exist except nothingness, he describes him not as the God 'who created', but 'who said.' This way, he is stressing the initiative of the Word – in the beginning was the Word. God is the one who made everything through the intelligent and loving communication of his Word. The principle is this: our life, our being, lies in the Word of God, not simply in a generic wish to exist; it lies in a Person who expresses himself in a meaningful and personal way, involving the person he created. This original nature of the Word means the original nature of the divine, personal initiative of love for human beings, expressed in dialogue.

– *'Let light shine out of darkness'*: according to the Greek variant chosen in the critical edition, certainly the most ancient version: 'From the darkness light will shine.'

Why is God described this way? We could have expected a different definition of God: the God of Abraham, the God who said to Abraham 'go from your country.' Paul prefers to refer his baptismal and missionary consciousness to the absolute origin, God as God, over and beyond any historical instances (Damascus, Antioch, etc). The instance is the unchanging divinity itself which deigned to show interest in us and establish us as the opportunity for his plan.

I believe that Paul's rock-solidness may be properly due to the fact that it is rooted in the unchanging being of God, where there is no 'why' to be sought, no new reasoning to apply, given that God is the origin of every 'why' and of every reasoning.

This way of pointing to the divine initiative leads our baptismal and mission consciousness back to the absolute nature of God before whom one can only listen, and there is nothing else. He is the *logos* of our being.

This reflection can be widened. The Word of God, who is at the origin of our baptismal and apostolic consciousness, is the Word of God the Creator and is therefore the root of awareness of every individual inasmuch as that individual is a human being. In arriving at this divine initiative, then, I can grasp humanity as such, every man and woman of this world, because they are rooted in the power of this same creative Word. I can grasp the created, loved and challenged human in myself which is identical to the human in every man and woman I meet.

This is the first reason why Paul makes reference here to God the Creator in order to describe himself.

The question could be explained further: Why did he not write, 'And God said he is the God who created man'? Why does he refer to the specific moment of light, light created from darkness? (This contrast closely recalls the way in which John presents the work of the Word in the prologue to his Gospel.) I believe Paul did it to indicate that the mission, and also baptism as the root of mission, presumes a world immersed in darkness, in evil. We note that Paul alters the Genesis text somewhat because he writes: 'of darkness' ('Let there be light' – Gn 1:3). It is clear that he wants to place himself within an historical perspective where, in a situation of sin, baptism and mission emerge as light. However, let's not take the description in too literal a sense: it is a way of expressing the reality of the dynamic of evil from which nobody is spared, because we are all subject to this same atmosphere, this corrupting degradation. There is not only the historical truth of original sin by which every person is born into sin: Paul seems to be saying that in some way, human beings are in the sphere of *actual* sin, in the lie which has been accepted and lived.

Besides the theological root of original sin, there is the fact that the world is eaten up by lack of meaning, corroded by insignificance, and struggles to extricate itself. It wants progress, human development, development generally, but this very desire is ruined by the insignificance of its attempts and its results. It is a view of the world which demands our ability to remain calm and to step back from it somewhat, because it is not always corroborated by everyday experience.

Thanks be to God, this is often good and gratifying, but it can be so destructive as to make us absolutely despair of the meaning of life. Through *epoké*, by gaining a certain distance from things, even someone not directly enlightened by the Spirit can achieve this perception of being a machine in a world corrupted by the fear that there is no meaning, seized by fear to the point of the most brutal absurdity, even the spectre of total war which suns up all the cruelty and injustice of history.

Nonetheless, the Spirit gives deep meaning to this view of the world so we can better understand the anxieties and afflictions of history. It is extremely important for apostolic consciousness, because it redeems us from the morass of gullibility and disappointments that come one after the other without our even realising how it is that we shift from infatuation with self or the environment, or what we are doing, to even more bitter disappointments still. It is a spiritual wisdom which is expressed concisely in the words: '... the God who said, "Let light shine out of darkness."' Knowledge of darkness through the grace of knowledge of the light: pure knowledge of darkness can produce desperation or presumption. The knowledge of the light that God makes spring from darkness ensures that we know darkness and the way of the light to which the world is called, even amidst the upheaval of its absurdity and non-meaning.

Explore this thought, one so fundamental to judging reality. I prefer to do it with words other than my own: I would risk allowing myself to be caught up in a very 'hot' issue today, because it is connected with the discernment the Church is making regarding the historical situation. So let me read out some words that express well what I feel. I am drawing them from the book *Sotto il segno dello Spirito*, by Fr

Francesco Rossi de Gasparis A profound expert on Judaism with a solid philosophical formation, he has been able to grasp very clearly certain aspects of contemporary reality:

> There is one objective which humanity today seems to find agreement on everywhere. This earthly objective is generally expressed in words that seem to encapsulate the most noble ambition that secular (not necessarily secularist), wisdom of this world has been able to achieve: to free man by humanising the world and society, its structures and its social and international relations.
>
> A great secular hope is thus exalted amid the multitudes and it succeeds in getting the hearts of many to quiver with a sincerity which only God can know and judge. The mature Christian, who is no longer fed with the milk of fleshly innocence, by people who feel they are exclusively human, will guard well against fighting a secular project of this kind for the freedom of human redemption. On the contrary, the mature Christian will take part in it, but well-armed with discretion, wisdom and language learned from the Spirit of God and clothed in God's armour. The Holy Spirit will teach such a person to discern, not confuse things.... The mature Christian remembers how many evils in the history of humanity and the Church have come from confusion of the psyche and spirit, words of Spirit with words of human wisdom, of undertakings aimed at the *polis* of men with those regarding the Church of God, the bride of Jesus. Confusion between ecclesial discourse and social

and political discourse has not only ruined some tasty dishes by offering them to diners who needed different food (Mt 7:6) but has often impoverished and made insipid the spiritual food the Christian community is in need of (cf. pp. 13 ff.).

Here, we touch on one of the basic issues of the Church's discernment in history, the specific nature of the journey of the *polis* and its generous efforts to achieve human freedom, as well as the specific nature of the ecclesial journal as one of becoming more Christ-like, a journey of human divinisation. The two projects are distinct, not opposed, and should not be confused. Confusion only generates more confusion, and we end up expressing material things in *spiritual* language or spiritual things in material language. Or we end up confusing means and ends, and sometimes confusing the minds of people with ministerial and apostolic responsibility in the Church.

Let me continue reading:

> To humanise the world with a view to liberating humankind, and even being involved in this task according to his or her understanding and capabilities, the disciple of Jesus allows people to work in a secular way with the sincerity they are capable of, yet is set apart by the spirit of God for a project of salvation and liberation of humankind which is properly divine and one that no secular eye, ear or heart can ever come to suspect or appreciate (cf. 1 Cor 2:9). God's saving work, in fact, does not hamper the work of self-liberation which humanity undertakes at a human level. It transcends it.

The formula for the divine plan of redemption totally transcends efforts at human liberation without contradicting or despising them. It can be put this way: liberating mankind by divinising mankind. Human wisdom urges people to get to work on the world, humanising it and thus freeing humanity. The divine Spirit goes to work on mankind, on individuals, to free the world (cf. pp. 16 ff.).

The light that will shine out of darkness is not simply one of harmonious development, better ordering of things, a better configuration of the world as it is: it is a new deed expressing the aspiration, need, desire of all those moving in darkness, and it grasps their genuineness, truth, spirit of sacrifice while also revealing the obscurity and ambiguity that pervade their efforts.

The ambiguity and terminal hollowness of purely human efforts to liberate history are expressed as follows:

The spirit of God gives new eyes to the believer to recognise how much the entire creation has been deprived of meaning and thus been enslaved by human sinfulness, individually and collectively. Far from being able to become humanisers of the world, to the extent to which they are sinners, human beings disproportionately increase pollution of creation around them, and this in turn continues to increase humanity's alienation. This diabolical circle of insignificance is also noticeable at the psychological and socio-political level up to a certain point, but its real, ultimate roots remain hidden to those who do not allow themselves to be instructed by the Word and the Spirit.

Human wisdom struggles in this spiral of death, looking for a sound point to pivot on and from which to depart to break the devastating logic of sin and its slavery. At times of individualistic celebration, it believes it can entrust the task to a single ideal human being, to the hero, secular prophet or wise leader (cf. 1 Cor 1:20). At times of collective delusion it believes it recognises the author of this ambitious project in the pure group, the sacred working class, in the Holy Church of the poor, marginalised and socially oppressed.

God's secret is that only the children of God in the New Testament sense are the true liberators of creation. Only the children of God, in fact, can give back to creation the meaning given it at the beginning by the Creator of everything, by virtue of the knowledge given them by the Word in which all things were made, and by the energy of holiness etched in them by the Spirit. Without this knowledge and strength, human beings can do nothing to unpollute creation from the toxic cloud of non-meaning and to liberate themselves in that order of salvation for which only the Spirit of God sets us apart.

It has been a lengthy quotation, but I truly believe these words can help us understand the profundity of the Pauline expressions 'light will shine out of darkness,' and can help us understand the future tense of that verb. This is a hope, a creative power of God, but introduced into humanity through

Christ, the first light of hope lit at the heart of history, and through those who allow themselves to be enlightened by Christ and become the light of hope for history.

2. God's action received by Paul

We can now more easily understand the verses that follow: '*who has shone in our hearts*.' This light, through which God has decided to save history tangled in the ambiguities of non-meaning, this light that is Christ, shines in the human heart to become a reality co-extensive with history.

We have spoken of baptismal roots of conversion, because the converted human being – who has accepted Christ as Lord of his or her life – shares in the enlightenment, the 'Christification' or divinisation of history. It is clear that by saying, 'shone in our hearts' – *ós élampsen en táis kardíais* – Paul is referring to the experience of his conversion to the light in which he saw the Risen Lord.

Nevertheless, it is baptismal enlightenment of every Christian, the enlightenment whose grace and beginnings are given to us in the sacrament of baptism and whose co-extension with life we celebrate throughout our lives by growing in our total belonging to Christ the Lord.

3. The action in its ministerial effect

It has shone '*to give the light of the knowledge of the glory of God in the face of Jesus Christ*': this is the apostolic goal of enlightenment. It is an eloquent expression and in need of word by word commentary.

There is the face of Christ, a human, historical face which allows the glory of God to shine through by showing the divinisation to which everyone is called. The purpose of apostolic life, of missionary commitment, is precisely that of making the divine being which shines through the face of the Christ-man, shine out through transformation of the heart in the face of every human being.

Every person can then express Christ in history, divinising it through their way of being and acting.

Let us ask Paul to be close to us in understanding the profundity of this message and, through his intercession, let us ask the Lord that what is in us through the grace of baptism may be shown in our actual awareness, that his Spirit gives us, of the grace we have received."

6

THINGS THAT OBSCURE
APOSTOLIC CONSCIOUSNESS

I would like to offer a reflection on the things that cloud and obscure apostolic awareness and what causes them.

The background that can enlighten our meditation is an episode once again narrated in Chapter 13 of Acts:

> Then Paul and his companions set sail from Paphos and came to Perga in Pamphylia. *John however, left them* and returned to Jerusalem; but they went on from Perga and came to Antioch in Pisidia (Acts 13:13-14).

Exegetes have speculated variously as to why John, also called Mark, left them. Probably he did not feel like going on, his courage had failed. That there might have been something negative in this gesture of John Mark's appears again in Acts 15 where Paul tells Barnabas:

> After some days, Paul said to Barnabas, 'Come, let us return and visit the believers in every city where we proclaimed the Word of God and see how they are going.' Barnabas wanted to take with him

John called Mark. But Paul decided not to take with
them one who had deserted them in Pamphylia and
had not accompanied them in the work (15:36-38).

Paul, then, had judged Mark's gesture as a backing away,
a diminishing of his apostolic consciousness. This gives us
to understand that such consciousness does not necessarily
grow in us, even if its specific development is something that
happens gradually.

The direction could be one of progress or regression,
of development or decay. Our apostolic and mission
consciousness should grow with life, but our experience
shows that it does not always happen this way.

The very inertia we experience at times is usually tied to a
lessening of the vigour of apostolic consciousness.

So, we are faced with a dilemma: either the vitality or
the decline of this consciousness. It can be important to ask
ourselves:

Why is it clouded: why does it not become clear as we
would like it to? Why does it become blocked and sometimes
even slip away? How do these mysterious and painful
processes happen?

The causes of this obscuring

I thought I would explain some of the causes I see from my
own personal experience to help you compare yourself with
them and find other similar ones in your own experience.

Clearly, everything depends on a focal point, as it would
appear from the reflections we have made and continue
to make on Paul's consciousness through the Acts of the
Apostles: the figure of Jesus Christ. Apostolic consciousness

is consciousness of being personally challenged by Christ and called by him. My apostolic consciousness is affirmed or distorted in real familiarity with Christ, by seizing hold of him as a reality of my life.

One needs to try, then, to identify the psychological, emotional situations in which the central relationship with Christ is dulled, keeping in mind that none of us is exempt from this risk, however mature in faith we might be.

(a) A first cause – yesterday we looked at it from the positive side – is *laziness in prayer*. This laziness is not only our absence from prayer times or the merely vocal recitation of prayers but is when we do not make the move from meditation to contemplation. There is nothing the devil fears more than occasions of real contemplative absorption, so he does everything possible to turn us off this.

We could almost say that the devil is not so much afraid of lengthy prayers or hours spent in church, but he does everything to see that we stop at a level of human reflection, so we do not arrive at the point where a person stands before God contemplating him alone, contemplating Christ in the totality of his gift, contemplating Eucharist, the crucified Christ. In fact, it is here that human beings succeed in grasping their authenticity, making it the measure of their clear and precise action.

Whoever does not achieve this authenticity and conforms to external rules, programmes or hastily drawn up possibilities, the result of reasoning, does not really have an impact on history, does not carry out God's plan.

We are often distrustful of the possibility of a truly personal relationship with Christ, do not believe we can arrive at the 'sublime knowledge' of Jesus which Paul came to and then take refuge in prayer as our activity, believing that being religious is the exercise of certain practices, without having the courage to seek out the very soul of prayer, that is, the gift of ourselves to Christ in pure faith and love, allowing ourselves to be taken over by his spirit to be offered to the Father.

Laziness in overcoming this step of prayer is certainly one of the important causes for which apostolic conscious is dulled in us, even though we read many books, know a lot about pastoral ministry and have great practical intuitions.

At a certain point we see that behind all our doing and speaking there is no deep motivation, and sense that it is just a question of skill, a well-learned trade, and perhaps then we begin to ask ourselves: why not use my talents in other things, commit myself to other areas, other sectors?

(b) *Laziness in disciplining our bodies* is another cause behind the dulling and obscuring of our apostolic consciousness. It is the person's psychological development, not religious outlook, that is in play here.

We need to accept our body as the place for and instrument of the Spirit's manifestation, so it is a matter of importance that our body be reasonably disciplined.

I am not referring to the specific discipline of chastity, and the discipline surrounding everything involving the structure and sexual regulation of our body: I am referring to everything that is discipline of the imagination, the passions, gestures, attitudes, use of time, food, sleep. Not caring about attentive discipline in these matters – our sense of balance and self-mastery – is harmful to the emergence of our apostolic consciousness, sometimes in quite important ways.

We need first of all to avoid reducing the issue to one of chastity, emotions, and convince ourselves that it is a much vaster one, though it remains very true that lack of sexual discipline quickly leads to the dulling of apostolic consciousness and deeper motivation; the dulling of prayer and giving ourselves to God.

Now we have broadened the question of bodiliness in general, let us say that we should encourage and gladly accept whatever maintains this discipline in us as part of the daily round, even though these things are not our doing, but are due to things like health, time, other circumstances. They help us adopt attitudes that will then be important for the rest of our lives. For example, there could be a problem with the time we go to bed, putting it off indefinitely so we never seem to get to bed on time. These kinds of things wreck our overall sense of a balanced lifestyle. It is clear that this balance differs from person to person. Each individual needs to discover the right balance, something we would normally achieve in our thirties or forties. Yet we do need to find it, and for this to happen we need to look for it, and to look for it we need to make some sacrifices, at times doing things that don't come spontaneously. Circumstances help, an austere lifestyle helps a lot, a relatively poor lifestyle helps too, though it is not enough: if this discipline does not become truly part of us, then our motivation and capacity for it quickly slackens and we soon end up with some unpleasant surprises in our own regard, discovering that we are rather different to how we thought we were.

In our meditation on Chapter 13 of Acts we have seen that it spoke of a community *'fasting'*. We could rightly call general discipline of the body, 'fasting'.

If we grow seriously at least in this kind of balance, we can recover it any time it is upset by things. Curiosity, wordiness, too much time spent talking about trivia, wasting time: all this is harmful, depending on character, and this is because we really cannot afford to play games with our body, as if it were like a diamond incapable of fragility and weakness.

(c) A cause involving our intellectual life, and which is often the root cause of lack of apostolic motivation, is *inadequate cultural development*. It can often begin with failures or disappointments not corresponding to expectations.

One could object that there is good will, there are virtues. The Lord shows us, though, that having made us human, gifted us with a body, intelligence, reason, he only calls us to serve him through development of what we already possess.

Inadequate cultural development is a cause of the dulling of apostolic consciousness especially in the complexity of pastoral activity where things often do not go as we would have liked. The people don't respond as we might have expected; we thought we had understood something but it turns out that something else emerges – someone with poor intellectual development is easily confused by this. Books, authorities we base ourselves on, do not explain what is happening; we think we are being misled by society, life, the Church because we are not accustomed to a proper understanding of the phenomena.

This could all be expressed as '*a lack of intellectual conversion*': there are things we have learned, repeated things, perhaps even really beautiful things, things in others that have pleased us, yet we have not managed to surmount the divide of critical capacity, the ability to critique things. The true apostle, though, must surmount it, must *at least* have learned truths even from false teachers so as not to trust every voice or bombastic, apparently well-constructed opinion.

It is certainly very difficult to achieve a mature critical capacity and we are all on the way to achieving it: this is why I said *at least*, learning at least to discern, mistrust, clarify, shift from naïve realism to critical realism.

Many people, although they have made this shift at a theoretical level, have not done so in practical terms, and still live *as if knowing were equivalent to seeing*. They manage their lives on the principle that we know what we see but, at a certain point, when we are dealing with deeper values, knowledge of God and Christ, this principle no longer holds. Not having understood that knowing does not only mean seeing with our eyes but responding to questions of meaning and value (a shift that marks human maturity!), they find themselves ill-at-ease when the world of religious sensibility, the environment, enthusiasm and success no longer accompanies them.

Not having grasped that the inner orientation of the person is what human beings are really about, they replace this with spiritualism, and after a period of purely mechanical and quantitative management of the religious phenomenon and pastoral involvement as well, declare their disillusionment.

The disappointment is keenly felt and terrible if the one experiencing it has not really and personally understood – and not just notionally – that human fate is decided internally, and that to speak to the human heart, to someone's freedom and will, means speaking to the deep core of that person's truth.

We could describe inadequate cultural development as a reason for the obscuring of apostolic consciousness in another way: *unconscious subjection to idols* of all kinds around us.

We know these idols well: the opinion of the group, the clan, the social setting we live in, our family or religious group, people's current opinion ('everyone is doing it!'), the ideas of occult persuaders and powers through media. We depend on these things, live among them and even express ourselves this way. However, it is one thing to live and express ourselves this way and quite another to be subjugated by them.

We are brought into subjection when something that goes against our current view blocks us and does not allow us to adopt a critical attitude to it, which clearly should be one of modesty, humility and common search.

Here, we are touching on a universal ill of humanity: the fundamental pessimism or realism regarding the capacity of the historical being to achieve truth. We think of the many racial, social, tribal, and historical prejudices that have accumulated, the many other prejudices that have marred free human choices. How do we explain the possibility of hatred, cruelty of groups of human beings toward one another, the terrible wars, other than by the web of prejudice, fear, misunderstanding, the ambiguities of existence?

Only an authoritative, unquestionable word, a word that draws on Revelation, can help us find a way out of this labyrinth. And since the apostle is called by vocation to collaborate with that Word, he must have developed an inwardly critical attitude toward the numerous *idola tribus, idola fori, idola theatri* saturating the atmosphere and involving so many people. The apostle needs to have experienced in the flesh the pain and suffering of critically surpassing common ways of speaking and thinking.

(d) *A subtle hypocrisy of life* is also a cause of the dulling, the obscuring of apostolic consciousness.

I say a 'subtle' hypocrisy, because it concerns a life which is already substantially good, one lived in a context of commitment, but which brings with it a discrepancy between saying and doing, perhaps because of the lofty ideals proposed.

If we are not concerned by this discrepancy and it is allowed to continue, it ends up by consuming apostolic awareness: subtle hypocrisy is a quiet poison. Small doses contaminate the existence of faith.

Nor do we resolve the discrepancy between saying and doing with another equally prejudicial attitude: the pretence of formal adjustments, adjustments which sometimes have the appearance of good, truth, necessity, but are nevertheless only partial, not comprehensive.

It is a complex phenomenon, even if we cannot spend too much time on it. But we need to get to a point where we no longer consider the discrepancy between what we say and what we do as normal, and no longer try to solve it with easy or immediate solutions or total rejection, solutions which after all are just formal adjustments and refuges for our conscience.

The truer and more laborious way forward is to recognise the discrepancy between saying and doing, between ideals and adjusting our way of living, and without pretending immediate correspondence between the real and the ideal, but not giving up on the possibility of this correspondence, by constantly asking ourselves: What step can I take *now* toward the goal? What step, simple but realistic though it may be, shows me I am on the way to the goal?

If we had to wait until we had achieved full identity between what we are suggesting and how we live, before we preach the gospel, we would probably never start! What is asked of us in order not to fall into this subtle hypocrisy is to constantly work on ourselves.

(e) The final cause, which brings us back to the first, is a *failure to grasp the central place of the kerygma.* By grasp, I mean giving real not just notional assent to it. Here, too, it is important to bear one question in mind: What does it mean to recognise the central place of the kerygma, that the Eucharist is central, that the Gospel is the original core of the entire Christian thing?

If we do not keep this question in mind we risk getting lost in the multiplicity of things, and, at a certain point, finding ourselves off-centre, without knowing clearly where we are or why, and how come we are doing one thing and not something else.

The causes I have indicated, and others you could point to, are in reality all forms of inadequate expression of our personal encounter with Christ, of his Lordship over our life. They take on different hues according to the various strata that make up our physical, psychological, intellectual selves and manifest themselves in a complex enough range of negative attitudes which stunt our profound awareness of the baptismal gift and apostolic call.

For individual reflection, after having meditated on these things, let us try to be open to contemplation. It does little good to evaluate our situation, question ourselves on the things that dim our own awareness, unless we succeed in praying as follows:

Lord Jesus, Son of God, have mercy on me, a sinner! Lord Jesus crucified, you know me and love me. Purify me inwardly!

Only you can enlighten and save me, leading me along the path to ever deeper communion with you.

Give me a true experience of yourself, one that is renewed daily so that I may grow in the awareness of belonging to you and no other, in the awareness of being continuously called and sent by you.

7

FIGURES OF APOSTOLIC CONSCIOUSNESS

We will try to reflect on exemplary figures of mission – or of mission consciousness in action – in the New Testament, so we can compare ourselves with them.

I speak of 'figures' in a formal sense, not of personalities, then, but of structural characteristics; and I understand the term 'mission' in its broad, deep sense of 'being sent'.

I am offering three reflections:

- Who these figures of mission are;
- What their activities are;
- Where they are passive.

Who these figures of mission are

I refer to a passage from the Letter to the Ephesians (4:11-12). However, let us read the entire context which begins with an exhortation from Paul:

> I therefore, the prisoner in the Lord, beg you to lead a life worthy of the calling to which you have been called, with all humility and gentleness, with patience, bearing with one another in love, making every effort to maintain the unity of the spirit in the bond of peace (Eph 4:1-3).

It is an exhortation to unity and with this exhortative background, Paul outlines a theological reflection on the unity of the Church, the system of salvation, and on divine unity itself:

> There is one body and one spirit, just as you were called to the one hope of your calling, one Lord, one faith, one baptism, one God and Father of all, who is above all and through all and in all (vv. 4-6).

From this vision of unity there comes multiplicity: 'But each of us was given grace according to the measure of Christ's gifts' (v. 7). Then comes the text we would like to take as our specific point of reference:

> The gifts he gave were that some would be apostles, some prophets, some evangelists, some pastors and teachers, to equip the saints for the work of ministry, for building up the body of Christ until all of us come to the unity of the faith and of knowledge of the Son of God, to maturity, to the measure of the full stature of Christ (vv. 11-13).

There are two fundamental realities being emphasised here:

(a) *A multiplicity of gifts and ministries corresponds to the unity of Church and the economy of salvation.* These two aspects seem to be held together; unity of the Church and of the economy of salvation, coming from divine unity (and hence unity of the community, parish, diocese, priesthood, the faithful) and the multiplicity of ministries. There is a tension between the one and the many.

(b) *There are five ministries designated in this passage* but we also know there are other lists of service in the Church (cf. 1 Cor 12:4; Rom 12:3-8).

I believe it is important to distinguish between ministries on which the community is based, and what we might call functional ministries, in the sense that they carry out some services in the life of the community, but also might not be there.

The text of the Letter to the Ephesians designates the founding ministries: apostles, prophets, evangelists, pastors, teachers.

We can ask ourselves then, what is the ministry of the bishop, priests and what are the other ministries on which the Church is based?

– Paul begins with the *apostles*. The *apostle* is someone who has the gift of the constituting and establishing the community, its foundation. He creates the link between the community and Christ.

In the historical circumstances of the Church, this seems to me to be the proper charism of the bishop. The bishop is either the founder of the Church (because the Church has missionary origins) or, in the case of an already founded Church, he is the one who guarantees that it is founded on doctrinal orthodoxy and orthopraxy in Christ, and who ensures the connection with Christ through apostolic succession, episcopal communion and communion with the Bishop of Rome.

– *The prophet* is the one who proclaims the Word of God for our time in an authoritative way.

– *The evangelist* is the one who offers first proclamation to those who are far from the Church. He proclaims the kerygma.

– *The pastor* is the one who guards and nurtures the flock which has already received the first proclamation of salvation.

– *The teacher* (theologian, scholar) is the one who instructs the people of God and makes them grow in Christian *wisdom* by exploring the connection between faith and culture, faith and civilisation.

1. *The first observation* to make is that the passage offers us some *founding charisms* and gives us an idea of their connection with the bishop, about their diversity, and a sense of how they complement one another.

Where do we recognise the priest in this charism? We are instinctively led to read the figure of the priest in the charism of the pastor. In our already founded Catholic communities the priest feels that one of his key functions in the pastoral role strictly understood that way, is to guard, nurture the flock and help it grow in faith, hope, works of charity, and hence in commitment of life.

Nevertheless, I believe it would be risky to completely identify the category of pastor as it is understood in Ephesians 4:11 with that of today's priest, because in a society like ours, a good part of it unbelieving and needing to be shaken up by the kerygmatic proclamation of salvation, there is a great need for evangelisers. Yes, the priest must be a pastor but he must also be an evangeliser, that is, able to proclaim the Word of God with authority, grasp the significance of contemporary lack of belief, be able to help the people live out the connection between faith and culture.

Should we say, then, that the priest should have a little of all the charisms?

Certainly. Just as the Bishop should exercise a little of all the ministries, but by reducing them to their foundation which is mission, so should every priest. Clearly, he will then be called upon to develop one or other of them. There are priests who have a greater pastoral leaning, others more capable as evangelisers, and yet others with a teaching ability and a real taste for that. What is important is not to stop at just the one figure: the Ephesians text presents us with many *figures of mission*, not just one.

While cultivating the qualities the Lord has given him, each should then always keep in mind the right relationship between the many functions. The priest-pastor who is the more important and statistically necessary figure today, will be a good priest-pastor if he respects the evangeliser and encourages this function in his community.

It is not even said that these functions should be exclusively carried out by priests: prophet, evangeliser, pastor and teacher are also lay functions.

The laity can certainly be teachers, prophets, as we see from the New Testament. They can also be evangelisers. Even the figure of the pastor, which in other New Testament scenarios seem to be more specifically priestly, does not exclude it being shared by a lay person, as a substitute or function of service.

The priest carries out these various functions responsibly, making explicit both the ones more congenial to him and those required by the circumstances of the Church.

(2) There is a *second observation* which is important to make concerning our passage and which is strictly bound up with the first.

The apostle is the foundation, and by definition this is *a mandate*, something he does out of obedience to another who sends him. Every priest who shares in the Bishop's mission shares in his obedience.

In real teams, this obedience is obedience to God's plan, people's needs, the task that historical service of the Church requires. *What is ultimately decisive for priestly service* is not what the priest is capable of doing, but *what God asks of him for the good of the people.*

This is a point we will return to.

(3) *The third observation* is that *all these gifts, these functions, have a single source: the risen Christ:*

> But each of us was given grace according to the measure of Christ's gift. Therefore it is said: 'When he ascended on high, he made captivity itself captive; he gave gifts to his people' (vv. 7-8).

Everything we are, both in our sharing in the founding ministries of the Church and as an expression of ministerial functions, we are from him, receive from him, understand in dialogue with him. We carry it out with the strength he gives us.

The activity of these figures of mission

I refer to already cited text where Peter says:

> … tend the flock of God that is in your charge, exercising the oversight, not under compulsion but *willingly*, as God would have you do it – not for sordid gain but largely. Do not lord it over those in your charge, but be examples to the flock (1 Pt 5:2-3).

Three features are presented here: *willingly,* eagerly, as examples. These are in contrast to three negatives: not under compulsion, not for sordid gain, not lording it over people.

This opens up huge opportunity for exploring the values evinced by these expressions. We will limit ourselves to the first: *willingly.* It seems very beautiful to me that this be said to priests, to those responsible as pastors and partly as evangelisers for new additions to the flock: do it willingly – *ekousíos* – as something that comes from within.

We have already seen what this 'willingly' means when we spoke of Paul preaching the Gospel 'not of his own will.' Here, however, I wish to recall an expression which parallels that of Peter's: we find it in the Letter to Philemon where Paul is writing to a friend, sending him his servant. He would have liked to keep the servant, assuming Philemon's agreement, but he writes: 'If I preferred to do nothing without your consent in order that your good deed might be voluntary – *katà ekoúsion* – and not something forced – *katà anánken*' (Philem v. 14).

These are the same two items placed in opposition in Peter's letter: 'not under compulsion but willingly.'

To understand the profundity of this willingness, consider what it is opposed to: *katà anánken*, as fate would have it. Fate is something we cannot avoid. It must happen, then we can do no less, and it is expressed in sentences like: I am condemned to doing this. I am trapped.

'Willingness', on the other hand, is expressed thus: I like doing it. I choose to do it. I like being a priest. And, if we dig a little deeper into this range of terms: I do it out of love. I do it in the Holy Spirit who is the beginning of the spontaneous fullness of true and free love. The *figure of the apostle's activity,* the activity of the pastor, evangelist, prophet and teacher, can be defined as the person who does these things willingly. From experience, we know how important this is in practice for our vocational commitment.

Vocations come from God's grace, but God normally sees that they arise when we meet someone who is gladly living out his calling, someone who expresses joy, spontaneity, relish because of it even amid suffering, difficulties, struggles.

On the contrary, incipient vocations are discouraged by examples of people whose vocation seems to be a burden to them, something no longer supported by the inner, supernatural zest that is the result of consolation and contemplation.

The word 'willingness' contains still more: it means doing things with a degree of fullness, completion. Speaking of ministries in his Letter to the Romans, Paul stresses:

> We have gifts that differ according to the grace given us; prophecy, in proportion to faith; ministry, in ministering; the teacher, in teaching; the exhorter, in exhortation; the giver, in generosity; the leader, in diligence; the compassionate, in cheerfulness (Rom 12:6-8).

Here, Paul is giving us a description of fullness, of someone who does things thoroughly, not in a mean-spirited, sluggish way which does not go beyond what is obliged, one's duty, what is timetabled. From a legal, formal point of view, the attitude of people who limit themselves strictly to duty cannot be reproached, but it is no longer the gift of Christ experienced in its fullness and it will attract no one. Conversely it ends up creating distrust, discomfort among people who see that it is a function being carried out in purely legal terms.

We find a further probing of this 'willingness' in the Letter to the Galatians, where Paul says that the 'fruit of the Spirit is love, joy, peace, patience, kindness, generosity, faithfulness, gentleness, self-control. There is no law against such things' (Gal 5:22-23). To be willing means to carry out one's ministry, one's function in the Holy Spirit, hence with love, joy, peace.

Let us examine ourselves seriously on this because it does not simply apply to your future ministry but the way you live your sense of mission today, and everything that makes it up: prayer, study, community life, apostolic services, attention to the poor and the sick. It is all an expression of the fullness that comes from consciousness of our mission and, beginning with baptismal grace, develops harmoniously into our priestly consciousness.

The passivity of these figures of mission

The reference text is one already quoted but it can now further enlighten us:

> If I proclaim the gospel, this gives me no ground for boasting, for an obligation is laid on me, and woe to me if I do not proclaim the gospel! For if I do this of my own will, I have a reward; but if not of my own will, I am entrusted with a commission. What then is my reward? Just this: that in my proclamation I may make the gospel free of charge, so as not to make full use of my rights in the gospel (1 Cor 9:16-18).

Paul claims that preaching the gospel is not a boast but a duty, a necessity. For Peter it was not according to need or compulsion. For Paul it is a need.

Between these two opposites lies the whole mystery of the apostolate which is choice, love, fullness, as well as something given to me by someone else. Paul picks up the word we have been trying to describe, negatively – need, fate, being forced (*anánke*) – and with much ardour he points to it as the root of his ministry. *It is an obligation laid on me: anánke gar moi epíkeitai.*

If I evangelise of my own initiative, I have a right to recompense (*ekòn* is the same word Peter uses: *ekoùsios*, willingly).

If I do not do it of my own initiative – *ei de ákon, the negation of Peter's ekoásios* – it is a job someone has entrusted to me – *oikonomían pepísteumai* – and it is because I have been deigned worthy by God to play a responsible part in the economy of salvation, in administering God's gifts. This is so great a thing that it concerns God alone and those whom God wishes to share it with.

So in an almost paradoxical way, Paul is expressing the side of the apostolic figure which is reception, having something entrusted to him, something not his own. Surely, you recall the parallel with the passage we have meditated on at length expressing the root of apostolic consciousness (Acts 13:2): 'Set apart for me Barnabas and Saul for the work to which I have called them.' It is a concept then taken up again at the end of the first Pauline mission where it says that they returned to Antioch where they were commended to the grace of God for the work that they had completed (Acts 14:26).

This is the mysterious, most important aspect which implies both spontaneity and obedience, the fullness of someone who carries out a work he likes, and the availability, submission of someone who carried out a work that is not his. Among other things, this aspect has a notable repercussion on the figure of mission which comes from it, something we can draw from Paul's Second Letter to the Corinthians where he says: 'Our competence is from God, who has made us competent to be ministers of a new covenant, not of letter but of spirit' (2 Cor 3:6). *Our ministry is a ministry of the Spirit.* It is God who has given us this ability, so we are able to be this way; he has made us servants not of the letter but of the Spirit. If this ministry came from us we could only express it as a ministry of the letter or of law: we would explain what has to be done, convince ourselves it is reasonable and just to act in a certain way, try to create conviction in the people, but just the same it is still a ministry of the letter. One can do it willingly out of an ethical or philosophical ideal: for example, I believe Socrates willingly taught his disciples how to move from a non-critical state to a critical one. I believe Plato willingly expressed man's yearning for beauty and fullness of life through his *Dialogues.*

We can also be convincing and more or less persuasive according to our natural abilities.

Instead, the ministry we are called to is service of the Spirit, service of the divine way of acting. It is not ultimately our task to convince, or to get people to act in a certain way, even if this is by way of preparation and readiness: *our task, ultimately, is to open people to the power of the Spirit of God,* to make room for the active presence of the Risen Lord.

I would like to stress how important this is for mission consciousness in today's world: if we were just ministers of the letter we would be teachers of ethics and ideals in a world which has little interest in ethics and ideals. We would be voices in the wilderness or defenders of a building that is collapsing. At times, when we hear some ways of saying things even within the Church, it almost seems like Christians are people struggling to prop up a huge dam about to collapse, using their hands and fingernails. The flood of immorality is engulfing us but we are the ones who will resist so long as the dam holds! This is the image of ministry of the letter, acting by conviction and persuasion.

In reality, we are ministers of the Spirit and can worry about the world no more than God worries about it because the apostle is no greater than the Master; the one sent is no greater than the one who sends him, but constantly refers to the one who sent him.

Awareness of ministry as something entrusted to us is the source of great liberating power and peace because it does not have us using a literal measure, which requires immediate success, but God's power as the measure, which is infallibly at work in history, in its own time and way.

The figure of passivity of the apostle is the figure of someone who *receives a service whose principal agent is the Risen Christ,* the Spirit of Christ. This is why I serve 'willingly', sacrifice myself with all my heart, knowing that God's work is greater than I am.

We often fail, stopping at one or other of these two aspects, ending up falling into either servitude of the letter, which is often bitter disappointment, or into a punctilious kind of spiritualism which at a certain point becomes a disembodiment of our acting 'willingly', gladly, and leaves us cold, alienated from the mystery of God just because we have not received it totally as a gift from someone else entrusted to us personally.

Lord Jesus, you alone know these things, and it is you who place them within us. We try to express them but sometimes we gain the impression that we obscure their meaning by using too many words.

We ask you to be the logos, *the meaning of these things in our lives.*

We know that it is extremely simple to live these things, since it is enough to accept the gift that you, Jesus give us, the gift par excellence *of your Spirit who renews our hearts and renews the face of the earth.*

8

PERSONALITIES OF MISSION
IN THE BIBLE

Lord, be the support of our words and actions since we are unable to speak the right words and we can make nothing clear unless you enlighten us with your clarity and unless the Father draws us by his power!

Grant that we may be your collaborators, abandoning everything to the work of the Father, so we can truly be apostles sent by you.

Mary, Mother of the Lord, help us to understand the spirit with which the Apostles worked. Grant that we may understand life as it really is and not let ourselves be fooled by false realities but can grasp the truth.

We have looked at figures in a formal sense, like a drawing with its key features. Now, I would like to invite you to reflect on figures as personalities in the history of salvation.

The text we can make most use of is the gallery of patriarchal figures described in the Letter to the Hebrews (Ch. 11). These men are some of the leaders, some of those sent, and we can read some of the characteristics of people on mission in each of them.

I will make use of a very simple approach: the interview. We will attempt to speak with these patriarchs, putting some questions to them.

———

Who are the patriarchs?

Let us begin by looking at who the patriarchs are. There are many of them, beginning with Abel, right down to all the suffering and persecuted people in the Old Testament who are also symbols of a persecuted community. But they are all presented as having an identical characteristic: they are *witnesses of faith*.

The author of Hebrews repeats one phrase seven times: *by faith*. By faith Abel; by faith Enoch; by faith Noah; by faith Abraham, by faith Jacob; by faith Joseph; by faith Moses.

These are all very different from one another but have nurtured one characteristic.

The reason is first of all that faith is connected with the exhortation the author is giving the community, where he says: 'Do not, therefore, abandon that confidence of yours … for you need endurance' (10:35-35) and then quotes the passage from Habbakuk that is central: 'but my righteous one will live by faith. My soul takes no pleasure in anyone who shrinks back.' (v. 38). He then continues, 'But we are not among those who shrink back and so are lost, but among *those who have faith* and so are saved' (v. 39).

It is from these people 'who have faith' that the gallery of patriarchs is presented as men for whom faith is strength, support, inner consciousness of a mission to be carried out in life and history.

A second reason for which the author seizes upon the unique characteristic of faith is that 'by faith' he means at least three quite distinct things:

(a) We can understand *faith in its more obscure sense*, that is, faith as a breaking with world by habits and expectation insofar as it obliges a person to do better, go beyond, throw himself blindly into something. Here faith seems to be far less concrete because it does not start from immediate expectations, daily calculations.)

(b) We can understand *faith as a reasonable thing*: seen in its continuity with the real hopes of human beings, with the best of human expectations along the journey of culture and growth.

(c) Finally, we can understand faith as *an enlightening thing*: the ocean of light we are immersed in when we abandon ourselves to the Sonship of Jesus, when we share in the fact that we are sons with Jesus and give ourselves up to the Father. We are then brought to a more exalted point of view which has us grasp the meaning of humanity's *concrete* journey.

This enlightening aspect of faith grasps the reason for faith's discontinuity when it is obscure, and the reason for faith's continuity when it is reasonable, by letting us see humanity and history from the point of view of Christ, the Son of the Father.

It is clear that 'concreteness' has three different meanings in these different understandings and experiences of faith. Obscure, opaque faith is opposed to an immediate, factual concreteness. Instead, reasonable faith shows a higher level of concreteness, of desires and expectations. Enlightening faith makes us understand that true, deep concreteness is the unity of the divine plan manifested in history toward its end point which is Christ and the City of God.

We need to grasp the *true meaning of concreteness in our life* and the true meaning of commitment in order not to allow ourselves be distracted by apparently clear and immediate meanings that are not the journey of faith. This is why reflection on this view of health is so important for understanding apostolic and mission consciousness.

Interviewing the patriarchs

What questions can we put to the patriarchs on the basis of the previous meditation, where we were trying to understand the diametrically opposed 'willingly' of Peter's and the 'under compulsion' of Paul's?

We could ask the patriarchs if they liked what they were doing; if they had difficulties; what helped them. And I believe that the profound meaning of the communion of saints will help us overcome the apparent futility of our procedure: the patriarchs are living men who intercede for us, listen to us, speak with us through the power of the Risen Lord.

I recall the vivid impression made on me when reading a conversation which took place in Toulouse between Jacques Maritain and the Little Brothers of Jesus. Speaking of the communion of saints, of our *conversatio in coelis*, he said that we do not always have the courage to live our communion with those who have achieved the fullness of their journey, and he invited them to reflect on the fact that in real terms the saints, especially those closest to us on earth, have intentions and wishes regarding us and we can ask them therefore to guide us on our journey.

The patriarchs had a great sense of responsibility for the people of God, so they certainly share in our experience with some trepidation and would like it to be authentic: this is the sense behind our questioning them.

Let us see about posing some questions to two of the best known patriarchs: Abraham and Moses.

(a) First of all, we will ask Abraham if he liked doing what he was doing and if he did so with relish.

I believe he would answer that he was not at all unhappy about being an adventurer of the Word. He always had the idea in his mind of travelling, since he was not the sedentary type. The Word had demanded plenty of detachment of him, had asked him to renounce many things, but had also responded to his cosmopolitan interests as a man of many lands, many tents and encampments.

But gradually, his wandering had become a burden to him: never one place, never a final land, always temporariness and precariousness. Even his progeny would be precarious because the son he finally had would have to be sacrificed. Abraham certainly suffered all these uncertainties and insecurities written into his history.

– What difficulty did he experience? The difficulty of continuing to believe in God, continuing to trust him without having anything concrete to show for it; the difficulty of relying on the divine promise alone.

– If we were to then ask Abraham what helped him he would reply that he was helped by the certain knowledge of the city to come: 'For he looked forward to the city that has foundations, whose architect and builder is God' (Heb 11:10). He not only trusted in the Word in a formal sense – the Word is the Word – but because it pointed out a goal to him which he saw as this great city in which there would finally be a home, security, abode, peace within its walls. Abraham knew he would never see it with his own eyes, but it was the true and substantial realisation of his desire and those of his people, and this is why he wanted to give his life, for all this. Certainty in the Word of God helped and sustained him over the days and nights of his wanderings to the promised land.

There is something else that helped Abraham: the fact that God himself was preparing this city. To the people it looked like Abraham was going here and there following pastures for his sheep. In reality, he was sustained by an inner goal, the city God allowed him to glimpse, which in New Testament language, we call the heavenly Jerusalem.

At the time Jerusalem was still a pagan place and Abraham could not have understood its destiny. But this city has shown itself to be the image of that very real city which is the goal of humanity's entire journey. All of humanity is called to cross the desert of loneliness and death and enter the heavenly Jerusalem, discovering its reality.

Abraham, then, was a man for whom 'faith is the assurance of things hoped for the conviction of things not seen' (Heb 11:1). His was an eschatological existence: the absolute clarity of the end was the measure for his steps and the immediate actions he carried out.

(b) *We can ask Moses the same questions:* Did you like what you were doing? What went against your will? What difficulties did you find and what helped you?

– Moses, too, would say that the move from being a shepherd in exile to being in charge of his people was not ultimately displeasing, because while peaceful, life as a shepherd was monotonous, lacking in stimulus and contacts. Once he was thrown amidst the tragedy of his people he felt a fullness and self-fulfilment he had never felt before. Moses felt all this as a great gift from God and 'willingly' lived out his role as leader, did so with relish.

– He would tell us, then, that the biggest difficulty he met was resistance from the people whose only substantial reality was the fleshpots of Egypt, unable to detach themselves from the benefits of their slavery, or to taste freedom, unable to see a way past the customs they had already received. Moses felt fatigue, disgust, anger to the point where sometimes he asked himself, when his people were seized by a feverish wish to return to Egypt, where he was leading his people. He would have said to himself: they are right to be crying out against me because I have taken the little they had from them and have not even been able to establish them as a free people! Why do I not just leave, abandon the lot?

– So, what helped Moses? 'By faith Moses, when he was grown up, refused to be called a son of Pharaoh's daughter, choosing rather to share ill-treatment with the people of God than to enjoy the fleeting pleasures of sin.' (Heb 11:24-25). The feeling of solidarity with his people helped him. He had chosen to be one of them and this brought him so many woes because he wanted to be *one of them*, but not subject *like them* to ease, laziness, habit. It would have been easy to be one like them or one outside them, returning to claim his privileges as the son of Pharaoh's daughter. Instead, he chose the effort of being *with* his people *on a journey* seeking to interpret the deeper desires the people had but did not understand, trying to explain to them that this was the real substance of life: setting out to follow their deepest desires.

Sometimes he had to shout, almost swear at them, whip the people to get them moving and this weighed heavily on him, but he wanted to feel united with his people and pull them along to their journey's end.

Other than this sense of solidarity, Moses was helped by another value: 'He considered abuse suffered for the Christ to be greater wealth than the treasures of Egypt, for he was looking ahead to the reward' (v. 26).

Moses tells us that in the final analysis he was helped by the abuse suffered by the Christ, the desire to be with him in his passion and his service dedicated to the Father to the very end.

How could he have said this if Christ had not yet come into the world?

Here, the author of the Letter is certainly making use of a kind of anticipation which is nonetheless not fanciful. Though confusedly, Moses sensed God's plan, the plan of suffering to achieve the goal, the plan Paul would explain by saying that Christ did not regard equality with God as something to be exploited, but emptied himself, taking the form of a slave being born in human likeness and being obedient even to death on the cross (cf. Phil 2:5-11). He grasped this because he felt that there was a constructive dynamic at work in his humiliation, loneliness, the antagonism he faced which would result in life and plenitude: his experience was that the dynamics of death at work in him – tiredness, heaviness, fatigue – only affected the outer man while inwardly he was being renewed daily.

Moses was looking ahead. Then come the most beautiful words of all: 'By faith he left Egypt, unafraid of the king's anger, for he persevered *as though he saw him who was invisible*' (v. 27). It was as if (Moses would tell us) I saw the end, the end of the journey, the promised land, the eternal city, the messianic place, the kingdom, the shalom of my people, the fullness of life with God, always being with Christ where God will be all things in all. I saw (Moses would continue) all this and faith immersed me in an ocean of light. I understood some flashes of it but the anticipation of these were enough for me to persevere on the long journey. 'He persevered' is *ekartéresen* in Greek, meaning 'fortified himself, took strength from.' Moses persevered, fortified and strengthened himself, consolidated his role through trials because his gaze was fixed on what was invisible.

Here, then, are some of the basic characteristics of these figures who were sent and kept their eye on the One who sent them, on the purpose and object of their mandate, the people.

Abraham says: the word of God who called me gave me strength, the vision of this city gave me strength.

Moses says: the fact of being sent to lead and guide these people forward gave me strength – the vision of the invisible is what gave me strength.

Questions for ourselves

Let me put a question to you: What is my sense of mission? At this point, how do I understand, grasp hold of my sense of mission rooted in faith?

We need to distinguish three senses of mission:

– The one we could call *the baptismal sense of mission*, that is, loving, dutiful, submission in Christ to the Father, which is the root of the baptismal call. Here, the meaning of mission is the fact that God loves me and has sent the Spirit of the Son to me who calls out: 'Father!' I am so loved and called that I am one with Christ.

– A personal sense of mission. In baptismal mission there is a mission which concerns me: we could call it *the confirming mission* (from Confirmation, the sacrament) which commits me to walking with others, expressing myself through service to others; not by my own choice even though I do so willingly as something I do, but as a mandate. The gradual loss of this sense of mandate results, as a consequence, in a loss of meaning in life – what am I doing here? If I do not nurture the deeper meaning of my existence, once the opportunities for amusement, relaxation, passing the time are exhausted, the drama of non-meaning flourishes under the influence maybe of great suffering, severe illness. This drama can even flourish in the life of the apostle in especially painful moments. We should not marvel at this since it is an extremely serious existential problem. Once sensible, real, immediate experiences are exhausted, one could well ask what sense there is in going on.

So, sensing our life as vocation is very important, even if it is not precisely defined: it is something already part of the mystery of God, God's love, and has historical, not simply transcendent meaning. It is a service to be carried out, a work of love, something constructive.

– *The sense of mission in this Church* through a mandate as deacon or priest. At this point, what is my sense of mission in this Church? Experience shows that when we are very close to decisive moments of priesthood, the most unimaginable questions arise: after so many years, do I truly have a vocation? At times, we find great difficulty in responding to that, because vocation is not something material and 'fixed'. God calls someone to immerse himself in his own historicity and face up to the risk.

Two kinds of concreteness are given us in history:

– *First*: I can make myself available, in an attitude of obedience and humble desire as well, for a vocation, whether or not I am ready and available before God is easily verifiable: I am or I am not available.

– *Second:* I can verify the call as an 'Antioch' type call. Someone other than myself – the Church, the bishop, those who represent Christ Jesus in this history of mine – says to me: Come! This is the decisive historical verification.

At worst, the bishop could also call someone who does not feel he has a vocation: I don't feel it, but if the bishop calls me I am ready. This would be enough to say: good, he is calling me. And since I am called, I say yes. Clearly the bishop will not call someone who has not shown a degree of availability over time, someone in whom some inner desire has not matured. The Spirit's voice, expressed by the Church, is decisive: 'Set apart for one Barnabas and Saul for the work to which I have called them.'

Not 'I approve of the choice of Barnabas and Saul,' but 'Set apart for me Barnabas and Saul for the work I, the Lord of history, have entrusted to them.'

We understand, then, how ecclesial and community-based our vocation is. It is not our little project: it is a way of servicing society and history, immersing ourselves in the dynamics of history which are the dynamics of mission. In fact, all of history is a mandate because its ultimate substance lies in Christ sent by the Father for human beings; it lies in Christ who brings entire humanity to its end, to the totality of salvation.

The spirit of mission requires a clarity and eschatological tendency which we are not accustomed to. It is often said at the Synod of Bishops that we preach so little today about eternal life. By contrast with times past when sermons always ended with a reminder of heaven and eternal life, today they almost always end with reference to the community and the journey the community must make. I believe it is important to grasp the unity that exists between these two: the reminder of call to eternal life is not about some great leap, skipping over the immediate situations we face. The appeal to the community, its responsibilities in society and history, is not really substantial if it is not part of the tendency toward the fullness of God's kingdom, of which the community experiences significant anticipations.

Let us ask the Holy Spirit for the ability to grasp the tendency that every human being, and everything that is more deeply and substantially human has toward the Kingdom of God, which we are called to be servants of.

9

JESUS AND THE FATHER

Lord Jesus crucified, grant that we may enter your heart and understand why you suffered death on the cross and how, through this love, you showed the world your relationship with the Father, your divine Sonship.

By entering into contemplation of the crucified Lord, we would like to understand a prime reality that constitutes Jesus' apostolic awareness and which can be expressed thus: Jesus and the Father.

Jesus sent by the Father

It is especially the Gospel according to John which reveals the mystery of the relationship between Jesus and the Father. In this meditation of ours, we will spend time with two verbs which recur in the Fourth Gospel and which mean 'to send'. They are the verbs *apostéllo* and *pempo,* and from a simple examination of them it is possible to see how Jesus' consciousness of being sent by the Father was alive and constant.

1. a) The verb *pempo* occurs at least 26 times in John, to indicate that Jesus feels he is 'sent'. In the conversation with the Samaritan woman, for example, he says to the disciples:

'My food is to do the will of him who sent me and complete his work' (Jn 4:34).

After the miracle of the healing of the paralytic at the pool, Jesus replies:

> I can do nothing on my own. As I hear, I judge: and my judgement is just, because I seek to do not my own will but the will of him who sent me (*pempantós*) (5:30).

What seems very clear is the intensity with which Jesus feels that his judgement is different from others and claims: I follow my judgement and do the will of him who sent me.

After the miracle of the multiplication of the loaves he says: 'for I have come down from heaven, not to do my own will, but the will of him *who sent me.*' This is the definition Jesus gives of himself. 'And this is the will of him who sent me, that I should lose nothing of all that he has given me, but raise it up on the last day' (6:38-39). Here, we can already see that the love Jesus has for the people is given him by the Father; it is entrusted to him by the Father and here too he is carrying out a mandate.

In a context of controversy in which he proclaims his mission, once again he says: 'I have not come on my own. But the *one who sent me* is true' (7:28).

And again: 'And *the one who sent me* is with me; he has not left me alone' (8:29).

This is a beautiful expression, because it shows us how Jesus experiences his consciousness of being sent also psychologically: in the various circumstances of his apostolate where he is in fact on his own, he does not feel abandoned.

In his commitment to the people he relies on the Father, the only one who can draw people to himself: 'No one can come to me unless drawn by the Father *who sent me*' (6:44).

These few quotes are sufficient for us to understand a profound reality that we sometimes do not consider. We see the person of Jesus almost in isolation, in his strength and capacity to decide. However, when he speaks of his secret, the secret lies in his abandoning of himself to the Father, in being the Son and feeling sustained, accompanied, moved by the Father. In all this, there is something very great that we struggle to really understand but in which the very mystery of our own person is manifested and revealed. Where do I achieve my authenticity? Where am I truly myself? Where is the root of my constancy, strength, apostolic courage? In my knowing that I am sent, supported, entrusted as a son to the Father, in my being in Christ the Son, sharing in his Sonship.

Perhaps it is a mystery we can understand in the eyes of the crucified Jesus: 'Grant, Father, that we may grasp this mystery that we never adequately understand but which makes us people in relationship with you, in loving dependency on you, people you hold in being, in action, at work.'

It is in contemplative prayer that this mystery emerges where the human being contemplates the sum of values, and himself in relationship with the Father, the creator and giver of life, truth, source of hope, activity, generosity, enthusiasm, fullness. The words we ought use are those of the Apostle Thomas: 'Show us the Father,' grant that we may contemplate you crucified, in such a way that we see in you the reflection, glory, presence of the Father, and may be in you. This is such a great gift that we should beg for it on our knees. I believe St Charles Borromeo prayed for it for hours in contemplation of the crucified Jesus and that he drew his strength from it.

b) There is a second use of the verb *pempo* in John's Gospel, and it refers to Jesus who sends, no longer to Jesus sent. Jesus is sent and sends: we are at the heart of mission. Who sends? The Spirit, because the dynamic of mission is inserted into the Trinitarian being. The Spirit is presented sometimes as sent by the Father and sometimes as sent by Jesus:

> When the Advocate comes, whom *I will send* to you from the Father, the Spirit of truth who comes from the Father, he will testify on my behalf. You also are to testify. (15:36).

Jesus reaches us through the Spirit, puts us in communion of mission with the Father and with Him, and makes us capable of witness.

Then the apostles are sent by Jesus. The fundamental text is John 20:21, Jesus' first words to his disciples after the resurrection: 'As the Father has sent me, so I send you.' The relationship between Jesus' being – his apostolic awareness of the apostles – and the Father, is expressed here in the most eloquent of ways and all our meditation can come down to this: the Father has sent me, I am sent, I do what he wants, and I am sending you. You, then, are sent by me, you have the awareness of being moved by me, of saying words I have you say. It is very interesting to highlight the fact that in the Greek text the verbs *apostéllo* and *pempo* are found: 'As the Father has sent me – kathós *apestalkén* me o patér – so I send you – kagó *pempo* umâs.'

The two verbs of the mandate are merged, one to indicate the Father's mandate to Jesus, the other to indicate the mission Jesus entrusts to his disciples. This mission chain is clearly extended to all those who listen to Jesus' words: 'Whoever receives one whom I send receives me; and whoever receives me receives him who sent me' (Jn 13:20).

We find this awareness of being sent in other great personalities of John's Gospel. The Baptist, speaking of his baptism and testimony says: 'I myself did not know him, but *the one who sent me – o pempas me –* to baptise with water, said to me, 'He on whom you see the Spirit descend and remain is the one who baptises with the Holy Spirit' (1:33). John feels that what he is doing has been given to him, and that what he says he has been told to reveal.

2. The verb *apostéllo* occurs 17 times in the Fourth Gospel. It is used to describe John the Baptist from the outset as 'a man sent from God' (*Jn 1:6*). The first presentation of a messenger of the Word, then, is the presentation of a mandate. *Apostéllo* occurs, as we have seen, along with *pempo* in *John 20:21*.

I will quote another two or three occurrences of the verb in especially significant texts:

> 'Indeed, God did not send the Son into the world
> to condemn the world, but in order that the world
> might be saved by him' (3:17).

Jesus' relationship with the Word, then, is based on the love of God who sends him.

Then, because they come directly from Jesus' mouth, there are the beautiful expressions found especially in the second part of the Gospel, where it speaks of Lazarus:

> Father, I thank you for having heard me. I knew
> that you always hear me, but I have said this for the
> sake of the crowd standing here, so that they may
> believe that you sent me (11:41-42).

Jesus turns directly to the Father as the One who sends him. This prayerful expression of Jesus' intimate awareness appears again later in a fuller way at the end of his discourse at the Last Supper:

> As you *have sent me* into the world so I *have sent them* into the world [kathós emé *apésteilas*]; and for their sakes I sanctify myself, so that they may also be sanctified in truth (17:18-19).

Jesus experiences a profound, intimate awareness of his mandate but also of being someone who sends others, because through this obedience and abiding in the Father's will, he saves the world and reaches every human being.

Lord, we find ourselves before a mystery which is not easy to grasp. We understand the meaning of the words, their sound, but beyond this we can perceive that it all leads us to the mystery of the Father, the ultimate, definitive and explanatory mystery of mankind. We praise and thank you for letting us share this mystery. However, we recognise that we merely stutter when faced with it and risk making it significant, translating it too simply and hastily into our language.

Grant us the grace of abiding in contemplation of yourself as crucified and of asking you what love drove to this extent! Grant that we may grasp how this love is shown by the Father, how it is a love of mission. Grant that we may enter into this love of mission even though it overturns and upsets our perspectives, our ways of thinking and being.

We always want to be the beginning and origin of something. Help us to understand that we can be so only by your will.

Each of us enters into truth, praise and gratitude only when we have recognised our creatureliness appreciatively, our being sent by the Being par excellence; only when we have existentially acknowledged that everything has been given us as gift, that being is a gift.

The sense of God and our creatureliness is what is most lacking in pagan awareness of man. It is the truth against which it reacts most of all, the fundamental temptation of Satan. The non-acceptance of our being loved by God, of our dependence on him, is the ultimate root of all our disorder, the disorder of society and history, and is the rejection that opens the door to lack of meaning in life.

Here, a profound conversion is asked of each of us, because instinctively the paganism which creates its own gods, which loves gods created by human beings, is continuously resurgent in us. There is no culture, no matter how outwardly Christian it may be, no tradition that is saved by this basic temptation which infiltrates all our works. Only the love of God, acknowledged, contemplated, accepted as the Holy Spirit, allows us to overcome this. Victory over the world is, ultimately, victory over the fear of being loved by the Father.

Let us ask the Lord that we may penetrate the radical profundity of this truth and understand how so many of the problems and psychological sufferings which psychoanalysis seeks to explain (often so impotently and lacking in results) have their origin in this essential point. It is not for nothing that John, who is the evangelist of the essential, seized upon it with such insistence and repeated it so often.

10

JESUS AND THE PEOPLE

Lord Jesus, we ask that we may contemplate you on the cross to understand how you looked upon the world from there! We would like to have some insight into this love for the people which your Father gave you, as well as your obedient and loving dedication to the Father through which and by which you are his Son.

This meditation is strictly tied to the previous one, where we sought to understand the relationship between Jesus and the Father, and the depth of his awareness of being sent. Now we would like to look at the relationship between Jesus and the people: What did Jesus mean by talking about 'those whom the Father gave me'? Where does Jesus' passion, unlimited love for the people come from? Why did he spend himself utterly, allow himself to be consumed for the people?

The passage we can refer to, among others, is from John's Gospel, where he says, when speaking of his apostolic awareness:

> And this is the will of him who sent me, that I should lose nothing of all that he has given me but raise it upon the last day (6:39).

Who are the people for us?

A preliminary reflection would be helpful, beginning with the question: who are 'the people' for me? Let me offer a personal answer to that. Up until four or five years ago, 'the people' were a somewhat precise group: students I was teaching, first of all. These were individuals deeply committed to the path of thorough scriptural understanding and as a group had grown to a thousand or more students from pretty much all around the world. Then there were the lecturers, study and research colleagues in other countries around the world: I would meet them at academic conferences in the various universities. These were the actual people with whom I had daily contact and from whom I acknowledge having received so much; much more than I was able to give them.

Beyond these individuals, and in the desire to extend my circle of relationships, I regularly went to a community in the suburb of Trastevere; there were young and old, lonely elderly people and the poor. They were pretty much from across the spectrum of suburban types, and I felt a keen passion to be with them, be part of their lives, visit them at home.

This inclination toward the people which is in each of us I was able to realise through these contacts, and I did so partly also through the experience of desire. So 'the people' also took on mythical features: but through the experience I had, these mythical features fell away and the people took on a real face.

When I was called to the episcopate, I feared that my contact with the people would be over. I would have indirect contact – or so I thought – and any direct contact would always be difficult for various reasons. In other words, I very much saw the risk of isolation as even a necessary consequence of the service with its demands.

I imagined that contact with the people would be through priests, the curial structures etc.

In reality, there was a huge surprise, because my experience of people broadened, and here I must testify to having received an immeasurable gift from God. The Lord gave me the gift of encountering a huge number of people through a census we held. What happened to me was something like what happened to Abraham and that God promised when he said, 'I will make your offspring as numerous as the sand on the seashore!' These words of God mean: I will surprise you. And the Lord surprised me by giving me a true relationship with more people than I could have dreamed of.

I say 'true' to indicate that we are talking about a relationship where the person, manifests as a person, a relationship freely established, not exploitable.

Now, when thinking about the people, I think of real faces which have become important to me, faces the Lord has given me in immediate rather than in generic form. They are the priests taken individually, people I can have real encounter with over and above purely functional ones, collaboration of mine in the truth of their individuality. Then there are the countless men and women of the diocese. I think of so many who write to me, for example, after having read one of my books, to tell me how much it resonated in them. This is a totally free relationship because I had never imagined these books would be written or would have circulated. To be honest, I was somewhat sceptical of this form of communication. Yet unknown to me, almost as if we were long-time friends, in a strictly spiritual relationship which always seems incredible to me.

I also think of contacts established with prisoners through deeply sincere letters. I think of the many young people I have met and who write to me. All this is an absolute gift: they are people given to me as a gift, those whom the Father has given me, verifying Jesus' words; it is the Father, not the imagination, or anxious anticipation, or myth-making I could make of the people, who gives me true contacts.

True contacts mean *serious* contacts. And (this is the rule) no one relationship is more serious than another.

The contact you can have with a worker, a hotel porter when you are heading for reception, has the same seriousness as one you can have with someone with whom you are discussing very important issues.

There is no difference because every person is a gift.

This testimony, by way of introduction, is an invitation for each of you to reflect on who and what are the people for you?

There is value, I believe, in the usual basic answer given by someone who accepts following Jesus through renunciation, and where the renunciation of celibacy comes into play: the people are not those whom I choose. The married state has a deep evangelical rigour to it and a need for greater holiness: but, it has an element of choice to it, some planning within God's overall design and in the name of his love. Instead, as a celibate I entrust myself completely to God for the choice of the people I come into true relationship with, including an emotional relationship with my existence.

This is entrusting oneself to the universal gift of God, availability to the totality of God where every relationship is a serious and determining one because the only fundamental relationship I have chosen is the one with Christ and his love for the Father. It is he who allows me to share in his love for the people, with the seriousness residing in every individual relationship. I believe that here lies the particular mystery of priestly celibacy: the confidence people can have in going to a priest whose binding relationship is his one with Christ, and who is able to be involved in the situation of the person who turns to him with absolute seriousness, not judging it as less important or peripheral.

Who are the people for Jesus?

The preliminary reflections I have made can introduce us to the analysis of some texts which could respond to the question: who are the people for Jesus?

We have already said that the people are those whom the Father gave him and who he must not lose since it is the Father who gave them to him.

I ask myself how the New Testament would translate the word *people:*

– *People* in the New Testament is the *cosmos*, the world populated by human beings, so the relationship between Jesus and the people is described by an expression of John's:

> For God so loved the world that he gave his only Son, so that everyone who believes in him may not perish but may have eternal life (Jn 3:16).

It is one of the translations of 'people': those whom God so loved that he gave his only Son for them. You see the totality here, no distinction, a totality in which all human beings know they are taken seriously by God, whoever they are.

– Another translation of *people* is *whomsoever, everyone*: 'This is indeed the will of my Father, that all who see the Son and believe in him may have eternal life; and I will raise them up on the last day' (Jn 6:40). The people in this totality and each taken individually as well: whoever sees the Son and believes, will have life. The universality of the gift is expressed, all the individuals whom Jesus has received in obedience to the Father.

– The *people* are also designated *symbolically* in the New Testament: for example, the *sheep* in the flock in Chapter 10 of John indicate the need the people have to be followed up, nurtured, led. A particular and specific task of the people is to be the object of Christ's pastoral charity. Maybe the decisive text for this is the following:

> I am the good shepherd. I know my own and my own know me. [I know my people and my people know me], just as the Father knows me and I know the Father. And I lay down my life for the sheep [for the people]. I have other sheep ([other people] who do not belong to this fold. I must bring them also, and they will listen to my voice. So there will be one flock, one shepherd. For this reason the Father loves me, because I lay down my life in order to take it up again (10:14-17).

The people are those whom Jesus loves so seriously that he gives his life for them. It is difficult to say more than this. We simply need to remain in contemplation of Jesus' love, and the abyss that separates us from his giving of himself.

– Another term in the New Testament to indicate the *people* is *crowd(s)*: 'When he saw the crowds, he had compassion for them, because they were harassed and helpless like sheep without a shepherd' (Mt 9:36). It is the anonymous crowd asking to become a flock, or people known and loved individually. It is the crowd that feels the need to shift from mythic and generic anonymity to being called by name.

All the words I have listed, and others, I leave to your research should be the object of much reflection. The prayer we can express is as follows:

Lord Jesus, grant that we may enter into your compassion. It is not simply a devotional welfare-type compassion, but the desire to share, be with the people. Jesus, we know that the very word 'share' can be an illusion. In fact, you want to make a flock of the people. You want them to set out on a journey. You love us not only for what we are but for what we are called to become: you read in us, the people, the destiny of life and love. This is true love, this is the nature of your shepherding and only you can allow us to share in it.

Jesus' love for the people is not static. It does not mythologise a certain condition: it is a dynamic love that takes the people in their misery, their anonymity, their loneliness, and beyond any labels or rewards, sees the journey he must invite them to take.

We should love the people in view of a journey, the goal of which is the heavenly Jerusalem, the plenitude of the City of God, the city built by God. We should love the people for what they are, because therein lies the mystery of what they are called to become, the mystery of the fullness of consciousness and the freedom of the children of God.

Jesus' lowering is a lowering that ascends. Is not he who descended, Paul would say, the same one who ascended far above all heavens to bring all the people with him? (cf. Eph 4:9-10).

Some specifics regarding the people

The New Testament has various specifications of people who make Jesus' love actual, make his pastoral charity real and specific.

There are many of these specific categories, some more frequent than others: sinners, the poor, the sick, the little ones.

Then there are categories which are there without being specifically designated. I would include women especially among these; Jesus' attention to women, I believe, it is a crucial point in pastoral activity and that maybe, as society is currently evolving, we are losing somewhat the sense of importance of women in the life of the Church.

We find other categories which we can translate into our terms as follows: workers, the marginalised, prisoners, the hungry, that is, people who need special attention. Among these I would also include the 'importune', people who make us waste time but are still 'people'.

We could also think of the mentally ill whom we must love and who show the suffering of society in a particular way.

There are the young with all their problems and the truth they express; there are the elderly, mothers of families, widows, singles.

At a certain point, 'the people' becomes a specific group and it would be interesting, for each of these categories, to gather up what the Gospel says about them. I will limit myself to a few passages to encourage your personal research.

– *Sinners*, are an extremely important category for Jesus. In terms of his own apostolic consciousness, Mark puts it this way: 'Those who are well have no need of a physician, but those who are sick; I have come to call not the righteous but sinner' (2:17). The sick here are the symbol of the human being inasmuch as that person is in need, and Jesus claims he is addressing the human being in need, weak (not powerful or capable), the person who is ontologically poor and in sin: that is, the human condition and God, in his mercy, loves it.

We are reminded each day at Mass of the substantial relationship between Jesus and us sinners: 'for this is the blood of the covenant which is poured out for many [another word for 'people'] for the forgiveness of sins' (Mt 26-28).

The Eucharist is his body and blood given for many people for the remission of sins. The category of sin indicates people who have not achieved their authentic selves, live amid division, discontentment, anxiety, with little meaning in their lives, in bleakness and banality: every person in whom God's glory does not shine through. This category is the object of Jesus' pastoral attention and love.

– *The poor*, those who are evangelised: 'The blind receive their sight, the lame walk, the lepers are cleansed, the deaf hear, the dead are raised and the poor have good news brought to them' (Mt 11:5). Hence, the native rapport Jesus has with the poor, the native rapport of the Church with the poor.

Many questions clearly arise here. In the Church's history the theme of the poor/poverty has given rise to may a controversy, beginning with the medieval controversies over the poverty of followers of Francis of Assisi, right down to modern theologies of liberation.

This comes to the fore like every gospel claim when it becomes the object of explicit attention and is sustained by precise and profound cultural research, otherwise it becomes our ideology.

The poor of whom Jesus speaks are those who don't count and know they don't count for many reasons: lack of money, power, prestige. They have a privileged relationship with the Gospel because the Gospel is God's power to which human beings open themselves when they cease to be proud of their power. Anyone who believes he is the origin of everything, does not trust in God. Instead, the poor recognise that they don't count and they become an important category for the Church. In its mission consciousness the Church has always felt a passionate interest in those who don't count in the eyes of the world, and it is through this passion that the Church is renewed and invigorated.

Naturally, it is not an easy passion. We can try thinking, for example, of what it means today to talk of real attention to pastoral charity for prisoners. When someone becomes involved in doing something for them, there is immediately division, suspicion, fear: fear that the legal principle may be broken, that lawlessness is being favoured. Yet, the prisoner is someone with a present, not just a past, so needs to be loved and assisted in his or her present, and in a difficult future. On the other hand, we know that the relationship with the prisoner must take account of passions that arise in prison, making it a place of worldliness and violence, almost a miniature repetition, a focused one at that, of all kinds of social degradation.

This is why attention shown to prisoners is so very demanding, and requires strength of mind, love and great evangelical courage.

– Another category which calls on Jesus' pastoral charity: the *little ones*: 'Truly, I tell you, just as you did it to one of the least of these who are members of my family, you did it to me' (Mt 25:40). The little ones are also the children, so often ruined and overlooked in their truth.

The little ones are people who have no sense of opportunity; annoying people, and the priest meets many of them!

The mentally ill require great patience and attach themselves to the priest more than others just because they instinctively feel he will not take them for a ride!

The little ones are people affected by various kinds of handicap which draw our attention and bring us much suffering. It is not unusual to hear of the murder of a handicapped person by a loved one, and it shows how, when faced with certain situations, people can be provoked into extreme actions.

So, the truth of a relationship with these brothers and sisters is a difficult one: it is difficult to understand them and live with them. It has happened to me, when visiting parishes, that I have gone to the home of a seriously handicapped person and have been left gasping at seeing the love of some relatives, some mothers. The mothers always ask for just one thing: to die one minute after their son or daughter has died! We think of the heroism of a man and woman who marry, presuming a serene future, then all of a sudden, their lives are transformed by this unforeseen event which obliges them to re-organise their lives. The priest encounters these 'little ones' in a true relationship. There could also be a fear that sometimes seizes me as a Bishop: are they true encounters? I believe that depends so much on us. The problem is whether I am true in such a way as to be able to establish a true relationship.

If we see that we are lazy, selfish, not so true, then we need to acknowledge our poverty and the need we have to be redeemed by Christ and let by him to genuine charity. Nevertheless, even a relationship that embarrasses me is a true relationship which struggles because I see that I am unable to help: the discovery of this inability, experienced in humility and sorrow, is the beginning of truthful relationships.

– Finally, the people for whom Jesus also has a name: *Israel* my people. It is a view that he sometimes expresses so drastically that it is frightening: 'I was sent only to the lost sheep of the house of Israel' (Mt 15:24). Jesus has his preferences and choices in his love, and Israel is a precise choice. Today too, attention to the Jewish people is an obligatory choice for the Church, a privileged attention which challenges the Church's family tree right to its roots, shaking it up internally.

Jesus' encounter with individuals

For Jesus, some people have real names: Peter, James, John, Andrew, Mary Magdalene, Martha, Bartimaeus. Or they maybe unnamed but pointed to as a class: 10 lepers, 2 blind men, the paralytic, the woman suffering from bleeding.

There is no encounter with people that is not a meeting with individuals. This is the ultimate aim of encounter which removes the labels, categories, mythical identifications and often brings us into contact with so much ordinariness, poverty, struggle, humanity. We think, for example, of what it means to walk through an Arab marketplace and smell the odour of the people! This is how people are, how we are; this is humanity as it moves through a very painful existential experience.

Only Jesus can give us the truth of these encounters and we must confess that we are still at the beginning of this journey, still needing to go a long way before we truly accept those whom the Lord has given us and continues to give us.

Each step must be a step forward and will be if we are true each day, beginning with the people closest to us. These too are people: the person doing a service for us, bringing the bread or milk, real people around us. It is when the indirect becomes direct that I am verified in my truth and not in my imagination and dreams.

Let us ask Jesus to immerse us from the cross in his love and mercy for the people, especially for sinners among whom, as Paul used to say, I am the first.

11

JESUS REBUILDS PETER'S APOSTOLIC CONSCIOUSNESS AND RECONFIRMS PAUL'S

In this final meditation, we would like to contemplate Jesus crucified and risen, at work in his Church, consoling and confirming it. In this way, we will lead ourselves back to our first reflection on Peter's hesitancy and Paul's strength. Let us now look at how Jesus rebuilds and confirms the two respectively and, we could also say, how he consoles ('consolation' in the technical New Testament sense of *paraclesis*) Peter and Paul.

Jesus consoles Peter

Peter had reached the point where he no longer knew who he was, knew not what he was saying, so no longer managed to have any idea of himself, of his identity. When he answers the person, who challenges him: 'Man, I do not know what you are talking about' (Lk 22:60), he is really saying he no longer knows who he is. Let us ask ourselves what Jesus does with this disciple reduced to a nervous wreck.

Jesus picks Peter up through love and recreates him, rebuilding his consciousness through an action that has three phases.

First at an emotional, wordless level; then through dialogue; finally, at a prophetic level.

(a) *At an emotional level*: 'The lord turned and looked at Peter' (Lk 22:61). Jesus stares at him for a moment and with just this gaze he communicates an infinity of messages to Peter.

We can very well guess what they were: reproach and attention, both; not scorn but encouragement and presence. Jesus is swamped amid terrible woes himself, and his own consciousness could well be burdened by so many other concerns, yet he looks attentively at Peter, and the verb phrase 'turned and looked at' indicates it was no casual glance. The apostle feels he is being looked at attentively, powerfully, and 'Peter remembered the word of the Lord.' Luke does not say that Peter first repented but that he *remembered*. This first rebuilding takes place at the level of memory, not rebuke.

Peter now begins to understand who he was, why this has happened to him, what he lacked (his presumptuousness, inability to trust) and is so shaken by it that – as the text tells us – 'he went out and wept bitterly.' The shock of this rediscovered consciousness is so strong. His memory had been shattered to the point where Peter no longer had a past or anything to refer to. He bursts into tears. The sense of rediscovered reference is his sin, his suspicion, the love with which he had been loved and warned.

It is naturally difficult to interpret Peter's weeping, because it says a myriad of things, but it is certain that it rebuilds him. Perhaps he thought: 'Look, this man is going to die for me, worm that I am. I betrayed him.' The memory of all the intimacy he had had with the Master rips him away from the confusion and inner bewilderment he had fallen into without understanding properly what he was doing or why.

This reconstruction at an emotional level, at the level of the roots of his consciousness is not enough, however. Jesus wants to lovingly continue this act of rebuilding.

(b) Now *the level of dialogue*, words, gestures, expressive modes which we can take from the scene described by John:

> When they had finished breakfast, Jesus said to Simon Peter, 'Simon, Son of John, do you love me more than these?' He said to him, 'Yes, Lord; you know that I love you.' Jesus said to him, 'Feed my lambs.' A second time he said to him, 'Simon, son of John, do you love me?' He said to him, 'Yes, Lord; you know that I love you.' Jesus said to him, 'Feed my sheep.' He said to him the third time, 'Simon, son of John, do You love me?' Peter felt hurt because he said to him the third time, 'Do you love me?' and he said to him, 'Lord, you know everything; You know that I love you.' Jesus said to him, 'Feed my sheep. Very truly I tell you, when you were younger you used to fasten your own belt and to go wherever you wished, but when you grow old, you will stretch out your hands and someone else will fasten a belt around you and take you where you do not wish to go.' (He said this to indicate the kind of death by which he would glorify God). And after this he said to him, 'Follow me' (Jn 21:15-19).

The level of dialogue is where Jesus has Peter re-utilise the fundamental characteristics of his apostolic consciousness which were shattered but which re-emerged at the basic emotional level though without being as yet re-expressed.

Thus, he reinstates, rehabilitates the apostle step by step, with infinite love.

How does he question him? We could have expected questions like: Why did you do this? What brought you to that point? Look, you were foolish and I had told you about it! A series of reproaches, then, to get him to clarify matters.

Or, over and above questions deploring his actions we could have expected others: Do you still feel you have any apostolic awareness? What are you going to do now? Will you succeed?

But Peter's poverty would not have been able to respond to questions like ours and this is why Jesus questions him about love: 'Do you love me?' The relationship is rebuilt at its most perfect and culminating moment, at its contemplative moment, we could say. Peter is brought back strongly to the day of his confession which was actually a contemplative affirmation. Having asked what the people were saying about him, Jesus said to his disciples: 'But, who do you say I am?' Peter answered him, 'You are the Messiah.' (Mk 8:29). Peter did not say: 'We say you are...' He did not reply with an observation at a meditative level but went straight to: *You* are the Christ!

Now Jesus allows him to return to that contemplative moment where the apostle rediscovers the 'you' of Jesus in all his intimacy, as the root of what he is and has been called to be. And this happens three times: do you like me, love me, are you my friend? Three times to point to what is the only important thing; three times to signify that Jesus has no other questions to put, that everything revolves around love.

We could ask ourselves why Jesus asked the first time: Do you love me *more than these?* (He left this last part off the next two times to focus on the essentials). I find it difficult to answer why Jesus said 'more than these.' The comparison does not really seem pertinent, but I explain it by the fact that Peter is being re-established as a pastor, responsible for others so must, where others are concerned, have a specific and very special intimacy with Jesus. Peter could have replied to Jesus' question in umpteen dozen ways: 'I am not worthy' would certainly be one possible response; 'now I have understood, it won't happen again…' Peter avoids both approaches, both depressing humility and the kind of self-assured security which could yet again sound presumptuous. He trusts Jesus. He has finally understood the lesson and replies: 'Lord, you know everything, you know that I love you.' *The root of his certainty that he loves the Lord, is God.*

With this reply Peter recognises that Jesus is the origin, source, certainty behind his love. 'You know I love you, you can read this love in me, you create it, you are putting it within me, giving it to me.' His consciousness is re-established along the same lines it had failed.

Let us try to consider whether we too might be led to penitence through this rebuilding of our person, not only through words, external encouragement or generic admonition! Let us see whether we might be led to penitence through an exercise that leads us to retrace our mistaken steps, rediscovering the right path! And let us see if we might be capable of helping others this way in the ministry of confession and spiritual dialogue: rebuilding people, being instruments of God's healing power, not simply by telling them to go in peace and think no more of it, but by saying: 'Let's go on a journey together.'

(c) Finally, Jesus reconstitutes Peter's apostolic consciousness at a *prophetic level*, and strongly so. We read this level in the verses that follow Peter's response.

We can immediately note that what Jesus says: 'someone else will fasten a belt around you and take you *where you do not wish to go*' is quite the opposite of the 'willingly' that Peter will use in his exhortation to the elders (1 Pt 5:2-3). Here, Peter experiences the tension that exists between the two ideas: if *willingly* indicates and will always indicate the *fullness* in Peter's life that God has filled him with, and how his ministry fulfils his life (this is the greatness of the truth of Peter's life), the ministry is *obedience* which will also be tough, dramatic, especially at the moment of martyrdom.

Jesus rebuilds, re-establishes Peter's consciousness not by soothing him but by telling him: 'You are full of enthusiasm now, full of generosity. I know that you are doing it willingly, that you love me and are my friend; however, remember that you are chosen, sent, that you are doing what someone else has given you to do.' Without hiding anything from him, Jesus re-establishes him on the way to the fullness of humanity that is a gift, self-fulfilment and also obedience: *self-fulfilment insofar as it is obedience.* 'Where you do not want to go' means even more: it is the promise that Peter will be like the Master who said: 'Not what I want but what you want.' The disciple is called to be close to those words of Jesus in Gethsemane, which he did not listen to at the time because he slept.

The re-establishment does not overlook this, does not make it any easier or trivialise it: it is a re-establishment of Peter in the strength and power of his mission.

Jesus confirms Paul

At first sight, it does not seem as if Paul had had a Gethsemane. Rather, do we have examples of strong apostolic consciousness on his part: we have already pointed to them and they could be explored especially by reflecting on his address at Miletus (Acts 20:17-35). Paul's awareness in that address reaches powerful levels of oratory.

Yet even Paul had his Gethsemanes, his moments of fear, angst, and every now and again he allows us to glimpse this. One of the more significant passages is the beginning of the Second Letter to Corinthians where he writes:

> We do not want you to be unaware, brothers and sisters, of the affliction we experienced in Asia: for we were so utterly, unbearably crushed that we despaired of life itself. Indeed, we felt that we had received the sentence of death so that we would rely not on ourselves but on God who raises the dead (1:8-9).

Paul had been harassed and threatened and had come to the point of saying: I can no longer go on. I have no more strength, am destroyed. They are very strong words and they leave an impression on us.

Then we see that Jesus is also concerned for Paul's sake and gives him some contemplative moments, so to speak, where he gives him new heart, reconfirms him, comforts him. There are more passages regarding this than we might think, in the New Testament. There is his first call, that first flash of light on the road to Damascus, which of itself could have been sufficient for his entire life. There are others that Paul himself recalls in his autobiographical speech:

After I had returned to Jerusalem and while I was praying in the temple, I fell into a trance and saw Jesus saying to me, 'Hurry and get out of Jerusalem quickly, because they will not accept your testimony about me.' And I said, 'Lord, they themselves know that in every synagogue I imprisoned and beat those who believed in you. And while the blood of your witness Stephen was shed, I myself was standing by, approving and keeping the coats of those who killed him.' Then he said to me, 'Go, for I will send you far away to the Gentiles' (Acts 22:17-21).

Paul is about to be expelled from the community, about to be removed, probably because he is disturbing the peace in Jerusalem. He is about to be exiled for more than ten years from the apostolate of the Churches, and Jesus gives him a fleeting moment of vision: 'I have a plan for you, I will send you to the Gentiles.' Even though more than ten years would pass before this came true Paul remembers it so much later, because it had certainly been one of the comforting moments in his life.

– In Corinth he would have another contemplative moment of comfort.

Things were going badly; they were in a mess. There were problems, and one night in a vision, the Lord tells Paul: 'Do not be afraid but speak and do not be silent; for I am with you, and no one will lay a hand on you to harm you, for there are many in this city who are my people' (Acts 18:9-10). They are words of huge comfort for a poor, frightened evangeliser who has already had to flee Athens and who begins all over again without knowing how things will go!

– A third time Jesus appears to Paul who is again in a difficult situation when he is about to be taken away from Jerusalem. He had been imprisoned, the trial was underway, and while he was in prison, the Lord stood near him and said: 'Keep up your courage! For just as you have testified for one in Jerusalem. So, must you bear witness also in Rome' (Acts 23:11).

Paul needed this comfort and the Lord gave it to him.

- Once again, during the shipwreck when all was about to be lost, Paul says:

> For last night there stood by me an angel of the God to whom I belong and whom I worship, and he said, 'Do not be afraid, Paul; you must stand before the emperor; and indeed, God has granted safety to all those who are sailing with you.' So, keep up your courage men, for I have faith in God that it will be exactly as I have been told. But we will have to run aground on some island. (Acts 27:23-26).

Paul, the prisoner, becomes the comforter of these people who are despairing because of the imminent shipwreck, and he becomes so because he in turn has been consoled by the Lord.

What does all this suggest? We cannot compare ourselves with Paul the Apostle, founder of Churches. Just the same, the meaning of the Scripture is that the Lord Jesus, whom we want to contemplate on the cross, and who is also the Risen Lord, will not fail to console those who are being tested. Perhaps it will be something very simple, a moment of inner enlightenment, a word from a friend, a sentence of the Gospel that will give us peace again. What is certain is that Jesus will comfort our apostolic consciousness at the most difficult moments.

It is up to us to give the Lord times and ways for listening to him which will allow, in all our bodiliness, for those circumstances where we can receive the comforting Word.

This is what we ask for one another in prayer.

CARLO MARIA MARTINI
Foundation

The Carlo Maria Martini Foundation came into existence through the initiative of the Italian Province of the Jesuits and with the involvement of the Archdiocese of Milan.

It aims at remembering Cardinal Carlo Maria Martini by promoting knowledge and study of his life and works and keeping alive the spirit that animated his commitment, encouraging experience and knowledge of the Word of God in the context of our contemporary culture.

With this in mind, the Foundation's role is spelt out in a number of specific actions:

- Bringing the Cardinal's works, writings and addresses together in an archive and promoting their study as well as encouraging and authorising their publication.
- Supporting and nurturing ecumenical and inter-religious dialogue, with civil society and non-believers as well, working closely together to understand the indissoluble connection between faith, justice and culture.
- Fostering the study of Scripture involving other disciplines, including spirituality and social sciences.
- Contributing to pastoral and formative projects valuing Ignatian pedagogy and addressed especially to the young.
- Supporting study of the meaning and extended practice of the Spiritual Exercises.

Those who wish to can contribute to the collection of materials (written, audio, video) on Cardinal Martini with by indicating initiatives regarding him by writing to
segretaria@fondazionecarlomariamartini.it

To subscribe to the newsletter (in Italian) and support the Foundation's activities: www.fondazionecarlomariamartini.it

BIBLICAL MEDITATIONS

A selection of sermons, retreats and meditation texts drawn from the vast work of Cardinal Martini. There is a roundup of biblical personalities from Old and New Testaments, explanations, some chosen topics to accompany reflections on the human being in search of God. The inestimable legacy of a man of prayer and contemporary spirituality.

1. **The Accounts of the Passion.** Meditations
2. **Paul.** In the midst of his ministry
3. **Our Father.** Do not heap up empty phrases
4. **The Apostles.** Men of peace and reconciliation
5. **Abraham.** Our father in faith
6. **Jesus.** Why he spoke in parables?
7. **Elijah.** The living God
8. **Stephen.** Servant and witness
9. **Peter.** Confessions
10. **Jacob.** A man's dream
11. **Jeremiah.** A prophetic voice in the city
12. **Israel.** A people on the move
13. **Samuel.** Religious and civil prophet
14. **Timothy.** Timothy's way

9 780648 230397